CONTENTS

ERRATA

On the cover of New Directions for Child and Adolescent Development,
no. 95, the order of editor names was incorrect. The correct order is as
follows:

Brett Laursen, William G. Graziano

Also, on page 50 of that same issue, the extract that begins, "Morality is
in many ways . . ." should also have included the following paragraph,
which begins, "Such similarities . . ."

EDITORS' NOTES

Over the past twenty-five years, researchers interested in the motivational underpinnings of school success have made great progress in understanding how factors other than intelligence contribute to children's academic performance. Largely due to theoretical advances in social cognition, we now appreciate the degree to which children's school performance is influenced by their beliefs and attitudes about learning (Bempechat, London, and Dweck, 1991; Nicholls, 1989; Weiner, 1994).

At the same time, there has also been a burgeoning interest in the cross-cultural roots of achievement and motivation. Several international comparisons have repeatedly documented the underachievement of American students as compared to their Asian and European counterparts (Beaton and others, 1996a, 1996b; Mullis, Dossey, Owen, and Phillips, 1991). In their efforts to place these achievement differences in cultural context, many researchers have been examining the ways in which culture exerts its unique influence on the socialization of academic achievement (Azuma, 1996; Befu, 1986; Greenfield, 1994).

This volume describes and critically examines the state of the art in research on achievement motivation in ethnically and culturally diverse groups. It addresses three visible shortcomings in the current literature—weaknesses that continue to hinder our progress, despite the collective efforts of a great many scholars. We have organized the book around three core theoretical and methodological areas, through which the chapter authors discuss their research programs and findings:

- *The problems inherent in decontextualized research.* The bulk of the literature in achievement motivation and school success is grounded in quantitative methods, in which hundreds or thousands of students have completed surveys and questionnaires or participated in experimentally manipulated learning experiences (Bempechat, Graham, and Jimenez, 1999; Bempechat, London, and Dweck, 1991; Hess, Chih-Miei, and McDevitt, 1987; Steinberg, Dornbusch, and Brown, 1992; Stevenson, Chen, and Lee, 1993). Although there is no doubt that research in this tradition has provided valuable insights into how children's achievement-related beliefs influence their achievement behavior in hypothetical situations or experimental procedures, the vast majority of what we know about children's motivation in the classroom is based on methods that are decontextualized. The chapter authors demonstrate the ways in which qualitative methods of inquiry reveal richly detailed portraits of achievement in school settings and, when used in combination with larger quantitative surveys, can illuminate nuances in children's perceptions of their educational experiences.

NEW DIRECTIONS FOR CHILD AND ADOLESCENT DEVELOPMENT, no. 96, Summer 2002 © Wiley Periodicals, Inc.

1

• *The need to consider culture authentically.* High achievement in diverse ethnic and cultural groups cannot be understood independent of the culture and contexts of learning. Recognizing this, many researchers have examined ethnic and cultural influences on students' achievement beliefs (Steinberg, Dornbusch, and Brown, 1992; Stevenson and Lee, 1990). Yet this work has gone on with relatively little consideration for advances in cultural anthropology, which has been arguing for researchers to consider meaning making in context (Bruner and Haste, 1987; Holloway and Minami, 1996). Ironically, some of the foremost research in this area has neglected to consider culture in truly meaningful ways (Bempechat and Drago-Severson, 1999). To the extent that different meanings are attached to critical constructs, such as effort and ability, we cannot know with any degree of certainty that the same question is interpreted in the same way by students from different ethnic and cultural groups. These difficulties reflect a fundamental neglect for the cultural construction of achievement beliefs, in the sense that many researchers have attempted to fit their findings to the ways in which Americans understand such achievement concepts as effort and ability.

• *The need to recognize differences within groups.* The generally monolithic approach to the study of culture and achievement has deprived us of the opportunity to understand what might distinguish students within a particular group. For example, while it has been helpful to know that relative to their American peers, Japanese and Chinese students tend, on average, to value effort more than innate ability, we have no idea how these Asian students differ from one another in the strength of their beliefs. Furthermore, we know virtually nothing about how these Asian students differ in their interpretations of the meanings of effort and ability (Stevenson and Stigler, 1992). The chapter authors propose directions for research that are aimed at building this knowledge base, which will allow us to move beyond ethnic and cultural stereotypes and toward a deeper understanding of the richly varied achievement beliefs of children from diverse ethnic and cultural backgrounds. As a group, we argue that our field needs to do more to embrace methods of inquiry that are qualitatively based (Corsaro, 1996) in order to develop a much greater understanding of achievement and motivation in context.

All of the chapter authors have been actively involved in studying the culture and contexts in which children's learning takes place. Working both independently and as a collaborative research team, we argue that qualitative methods of inquiry, alone or in combination with quantitative methods, can successfully address these needs.

In Chapter Two, Susan Holloway and Kazuko Behrens examine a puzzling issue in the research on Japanese mothers' self-perceptions of their parenting skills. In international comparisons based on qualitative assessments, Japanese mothers are generally viewed as exceptionally responsive to their children when they are quite young and as effective in supporting them as they progress through school. Yet, surprisingly, when asked to report their self-efficacy as mothers, they express little confidence in their ability to be an effective parent. Holloway and Behrens take this apparent paradox as a starting point. Their assumption is that although perceptions of efficacy are an important component affecting mothers' behavior toward their children, the meaning of self-efficacy may be particular to the Japanese context. In addition, the determinants of efficacy, and the ways in which it manifests itself in parenting behavior, also vary by culture. They argue that qualitative work is essential to understanding how the construct of efficacy works within the context of parenting in home and school settings in Japan. Specifically, they highlight the contributions that a qualitative approach can make to the understanding of cognitive representations related to parenting.

In Chapter Three, Jin Li notes that despite much cross-cultural research on achievement motivation and school performance, we know little about how members of cultures conceptualize learning and achievement. Li argues that there are at least three reasons for this gap. First, we have tended to rely heavily on preconceived, etic notions about learning and achievement, derived from Western traditional experimental research and applied straightforwardly to other cultures, often without regard to their emic perspectives. Second, we have tended to overemphasize discrete phenomena (such as success and ability) and specific tasks (for example, solving a puzzle) at the cost of larger contexts and systems (what learning and achievement may mean to people personally, for instance). Third, a dichotomous conceptual framework (for example, success versus failure, ability versus effort, and intrinsic versus extrinsic interest) has been dominating research on learning and achievement. Human learning and achievement experiences rarely involve only these polar ends.

Li presents a new line of research, guided by two research questions: How do people in different cultures think about learning? and How are their conceptions organized as a whole? Using prototype methods of cognitive science to collect free associations of learning-related words and phrases in both Chinese and American English from college seniors, Li presents a map for each culture's conceptualization of learning, which she refers to as cultural models of learning. Li reveals that although both cultures have an equally complex model of learning, there is little overlap in specific meanings and their organizations. She argues that in order to advance our understanding of how human beings learn, how children develop ideas about learning, and how they ultimately achieve, we must reexamine these domains as people define and experience them in their own social and cultural contexts.

In Chapter Four, Neil Hufton, Julian Elliott, and Leonid Illushin call for culturally sensitive, multimethod approaches in which individual meaning making is emphasized as a key element in gaining greater understanding of motivational contexts. Their research on motivation and education practice in Sunderland (United Kingdom), St. Petersburg (Russia), and eastern Kentucky (United States) has revealed a number of puzzling findings.

For example, despite a more critical and admonitory stance on the part of Russian teachers, with far less emphasis on the inculcation of self-esteem, students in St. Petersburg report a more favorable orientation toward school and a greater liking for their teachers. Western students' greater sense of academic self-efficacy, as suggested by survey and interview data, is not reflected by classroom observations. In addition, teenagers in Kentucky and Sunderland placed greater stress on effort than ability in determining achievement, yet such attributions appeared not to result in higher work rates. Russian teenagers stressed ability above effort yet appeared to work harder, both at home and in class, than their Western peers. Hufton, Elliott, and Illushin explore these and other puzzling findings and argue that they demonstrate the limitations of current theories and methodology in the field of motivation in education. In particular, they suggest that many constructs, including self-esteem, academic achievement, intrinsic and extrinsic motivation, and effort, cannot be easily considered in decontextualized value-free fashion.

In Chapter Five, Gisell Quihuis, Janine Bempechat, Norma Jimenez, and Beth Boulay note that despite more than two decades of study on children's theories of intelligence, the research has yet to address students' *own* understandings of the rigidity (termed entity theory) or malleability (termed incremental theory) of intelligence. Rather, the theories of intelligence said to be held by children have, in fact, been externally imposed by researchers. Quihuis and her colleagues report the results of a study that examined the relationship between students' theory classifications (entity or incremental) and their emic understandings of these constructs in the context of their schooling experiences.

Their study combined quantitative and qualitative methodologies to examine students' implicit theories of intelligence and the meanings they attach to these theories in four academic domains. Regardless of their classification as entity or incremental theorists, all the students, when given the opportunity to speak about views, asserted positions consistent with an incremental theory and articulated mastery-oriented strategies ordinarily associated with incremental beliefs. These authors argue that there is a pressing need for the field to move toward qualitative methods in order to understand how individual meaning making influences students' learning in the classroom.

In Chapter Six, Robert LeVine draws on research in cultural anthropology and cultural psychology to place the current movement toward qualitative methods of inquiry in historical perspective. LeVine argues that the psychosocial bases of achievement motivation, when integrated with principles of cultural anthropology and cultural psychology, will move forward in both theory and research. Specifically, he integrates the research findings presented in the previous chapters and discusses directions for future research.

The chapter authors have pulled together the threads from their cross-national and cross-ethnic studies of motivation to identify a number of methodological weaknesses. They point to gaps in the literature and conclude by calling for new, multiple methodologies that are authentic and contextualized and examine differences in students' beliefs and experiences, both internationally and intranationally. It is far easier, however, to identify conceptual and methodological weaknesses and offer suggestions for future investigations than it is to realize these in actuality. In response to the challenges they set out here, the authors are planning a collaborative cross-cultural and cross-ethnic investigation that seeks to avoid many of the difficulties they highlight in this volume. Operationalizing key methodological principles in the ways we have outlined has proven to be a complex and demanding task. Yet in persisting with this, we are reminded of the words of H. L. Mencken: "For every complex problem, there is a simple solution that is simple, neat, and wrong."

Janine Bempechat
Julian G. Elliott
Editors

References

Azuma, H. "Cross-National Research in Child Development: The Hess-Azuma Collaboration in Retrospect." In D. W. Shwalb and B. J. Shwalb (eds.), *Japanese Childrearing: Two Generations of Scholarship*. New York: Guilford Press, 1996.

Beaton, A. E., and others. *Mathematics Achievement in the Middle School Years: IEA's Third International Mathematics and Science Study (TIMSS)*. Boston: Center for the Study of Testing, Evaluation, and Educational Policy, Boston College, 1996a.

Beaton, A. E., and others. *Science Achievement in the Middle School Years: IEA's Third International Mathematics and Science Study (TIMSS)*. Boston: Center for the Study of Testing, Evaluation, and Educational Policy, Boston College, 1996b.

Befu, H. "The Social and Cultural Background of Child Development in Japan and the United States." In H. Stevenson, H. Azuma, and K. Hakuta (eds.), *Child Development and Education in Japan*. New York: Freeman, 1986.

Bempechat, J., and Drago-Severson, E. "Cross-National Differences in Academic Achievement: Beyond Etic Conceptions of Children's Understandings." *Review of Educational Research*, 1999, *69*, 287–314.

Bempechat, J., Graham, S., and Jimenez, N. "The Socialization of Achievement in Poor and Minority Students: A Comparative Study." *Journal of Cross-Cultural Psychology*, 1999, *30*, 139–158.

Bempechat, J., London, P., and Dweck, C. S. "Children's Conceptions of Ability in Major Domains: An Interview and Experimental Study." *Child Study Journal*, 1991, *21*, 11–35.

Bruner, J., and Haste, H. *Making Sense: The Child's Construction of the World*. London: Methuen, 1987.

Corsaro, W. "Transitions in Early Childhood: The Promise of Comparative, Longitudinal Ethnography." In R. Jessor, A. Colby, and R. A. Shweder (eds.), *Ethnography and Human Development: Context and Meaning in Social Inquiry*. Chicago: University of Chicago Press, 1996.

Greenfield, P. M. "Independence and Interdependence as Developmental Scripts: Implications for Theory, Research, and Practice." In P. M. Greenfield and R. R. Cocking (eds.), *Cross-Cultural Roots of Minority Child Development*. Mahwah, N.J.: Erlbaum, 1994.

Hess, R. D., Chih-Miei, C., and McDevitt, T. M. "Cultural Variations in Family Beliefs About Children's Performance in Mathematics: Comparisons Among People's Republic of China, Chinese-American, and Caucasian-American Families." *Journal of Educational Psychology, 1987, 79,* 179–188.

Holloway, S., and Minami, M. "Production and Reproduction of Culture: The Dynamic Role of Mothers and Children in Early Socialization." In D. W. Shwalb and B. J. Shwalb (eds.), *Japanese Childrearing: Two Generations of Scholarship*. New York: Guilford Press, 1996.

Mullis, I., Dossey, J., Owen, E., and Phillips, G. *The State of Mathematics Achievement.* Washington, D.C.: National Center for Education Statistics, 1991.

Nicholls, J. G. *The Democratic Ethos and Competitive Education.* Cambridge, Mass.: Harvard University Press, 1989.

Steinberg, L., Dornbusch, S., and Brown, B. "Ethnic Differences in Adolescent Achievement: An Ecological Perspective." *American Psychologist, 1992, 47,* 723–729.

Stevenson, H., Chen, C., and Lee, S. "Mathematics Achievement of Chinese, Japanese, and American Children: Ten Years Later." *Science, 1993, 259,* 53–58.

Stevenson, H. W., and Lee, S. Y. "Contexts of Achievement: A Study of American, Chinese, and Japanese Children." *Monographs of the Society for Research in Child Development, 1990, 55*(1–2). Serial no. 221.

Stevenson, H. W., and Stigler, J. W. *The Learning Gap: Why Our Schools Are Failing and What We Can Learn from Japanese and Chinese Education.* New York: Simon & Schuster, 1992.

Weiner, B. "Integrating Social and Personal Theories of Achievement Strivings." *Review of Educational Research, 1994, 64,* 557–573.

JANINE BEMPECHAT is senior consultant at the Program for Educational Change Agents, Eliot-Pearson Department of Child Development, Tufts University, Medford, Massachusetts.

JULIAN G. ELLIOTT is professor of educational psychology and associate dean at the School of Education, University of Sunderland, England.

1

To make progress in understanding the ways in which students' achievement beliefs influence their achievement behavior, we need to design investigations that contextualize research questions and pay explicit attention to within-group differences.

The Culture and Contexts of Achievement Motivation

Julian G. Elliott, Janine Bempechat

We are at a crossroad in cross-ethnic and cross-cultural research on children's motivation to achieve. The research of the past quarter-century has remained somewhat stagnant and embedded in traditional methods of inquiry, the most common of which are experimental studies and large-scale surveys of children's, parents', and teachers' beliefs about learning and achievement. The result is that we have a rather extensive literature on, for example, the ways in which children's intrinsic desire to learn is differentially affected by varied reward conditions and different ways that success or failure can be induced to produce a variety of reactions to success or failure. As a result of the considerable efforts of the International Association for Educational Achievement (IEA), whose most recent works are the Third International Mathematics and Science Study (TIMSS) (Beaton and others, 1996a, 1996b) and TIMSS-R (Martin and others, 2000; Mullis and others, 2000), we also know what thousands of students in over forty industrialized nations think about the causes of success and failure and the value of mathematics and science in their daily lives.

Our goal here is not to minimize the advances in knowledge that have benefited all of us, researchers and educators alike. Indeed, each of the chapter authors in this volume has learned from and contributed to the work we now find in need of new directions. Rather, we wish to demonstrate that the time is ripe to embrace mixed or hybrid methods of inquiry. In other words, we believe that we can move the field forward by conducting research that is contextualized, authentic, and mindful of differences within groups of children, parents, and teachers.

In this chapter, we examine what this means to both researchers and practitioners. We present specific examples from our own work that demonstrate how cross-cultural and cross-ethnic research can come to have more meaning to those constituents who have a vested interest in improving children's desire to do well in school.

Children's Motivation to Achieve: From Inner Drive to Interpretive Beliefs

The emergence and development of social cognition as an organizing theory has had a major impact on research in achievement motivation. The overarching theoretical principle is that inasmuch as children's social behavior is influenced by their cognitive development, the latter is very much influenced by their social interactions. This realization of a mutual relationship between cognition and social behavior led researchers to inquire about the ways in which children's beliefs about learning might influence their achievement behavior in the classroom. Largely as a result of Bernard Weiner's work, we have gone from viewing achievement as emanating from an inner need or drive, to investigating the extent to which the relationship between the need for achievement and achievement-related behavior is mediated by achievement cognitions, including affect, confidence, expectancies, and beliefs about the nature of intelligence (Weiner, 1972, 1994; Weiner, Graham, Stern, and Lawson, 1982; Weiner, Russell, and Lerman, 1979).

This theoretical advance paved the way for an extensive body of literature that has identified a variety of home, school, classroom, peer, and community factors, each with a unique influence on how children think about their learning experiences. A great deal of research has been experimental in nature. For example, Ames's studies of the influence of classroom structure on children's achievement beliefs helped to advance U.S. discourse on competitive as compared to cooperative learning (Ames and Archer, 1987; Ames and Ames, 1984). Specifically, her experimental studies showed that under competitive conditions, in which two children know that the one who solves more problems will receive a prize, concerns about ability become more salient, the "successful" student develops inflated views of his or her ability, and the "unsuccessful" student becomes self-deprecating. Under cooperative conditions, in which the "group" (which is composed of two children) succeeds in winning the prize, evaluations of the less able become elevated. However, under conditions that cause the "group" to fail, evaluations of the less able become very negative. This kind of work led practitioners to reevaluate the ways in which they organize their classrooms around cooperative learning. For example, Slavin's work revealed that cooperative learning is not simply a matter of assigning children to work on a particular project. He demonstrated that in order for a number of children to work successfully as a group, teachers must mandate individual responsibility and accountability (Slavin, 1991).

A variety of questionnaire studies have examined the relationship between academic achievement and achievement-related beliefs, such as academic self-esteem and attributions for success and failure (Bempechat, Nakkula, Wu, and Ginsburg, 1996; Eccles, 1993; Holloway, Kashiwagi, Hess, and Azuma, 1986; Marsh and Yeung, 1997). For example, there is strong evidence that higher-achieving students attribute their success in school to ability and do not believe that failure or setbacks are the result of lack of ability (Bempechat, Nakkula, Wu, and Ginsburg, 1996; Dweck, 1975; Eccles (Parsons), Adler, and Meece, 1984; Eccles and Wigfield, 1995; Harter and Connell, 1984; Marsh, 1984; Marsh and others, 1984; Stipek and Hoffman, 1980; Wolleat, Pedro, Becker, and Fennema, 1980; Wylie, 1979).

In contrast, lower-achieving students tend to attribute failure to lack of ability, a potentially debilitating belief (Bempechat, Nakkula, Wu, and Ginsburg, 1996; Marsh, 1984; Marsh and others, 1984). As Weiner (1982, 1994) has demonstrated, most students perceive lack of ability as an attribute that is internal, relatively stable, and one over which they have little or no control. The implication is that effort is unlikely to result in any meaningful improvement in performance, thus fostering the kind of disengagement in learning that parents and teachers work so hard to discourage.

Of course, these kinds of studies cannot address issues of causality. It could be that students who do well in school come to believe that they have high ability. Alternatively, it could very well be that perceptions of high ability foster higher achievement in school. This is an issue that visits every correlational study and is the primary reason that researchers remain cautious in the interpretations they bring to bear on their findings.

The reader may well ask what the relationship is between attributions to effort and academic achievement. It makes intuitive sense that higher-achieving students would also attribute success to effort and failure to lack of effort. Regrettably, the methods used to assess attributions have failed to reveal such a relationship. This does not mean that it does not exist. It means simply that the questionnaires we typically use to assess the relationship between students' beliefs about the causes of success and failure and academic achievement do not ferret out such relationships. This shortcoming speaks directly to our belief that surveys must be complemented by individual interviews, so that such intuitive relationships can be explored.

Cross-National Studies of Academic Achievement: Asian and American Performance

Interestingly, the accumulated literature on cross-national differences in mathematics and science achievement has dovetailed very nicely with research in achievement motivation. In the early 1980s, when the first studies revealed that American students lagged well behind their Japanese, Chinese, and Taiwanese peers in mathematics and science achievement

(Stevenson, Chen, and Lee, 1993; Stevenson, Lee, and Stigler, 1986), investigators naturally wanted to gain greater understanding and thus began to examine home, school, and individual differences that might account for such discrepancies.

Mothers' and students' beliefs about the causes of success and failure became the most prominently studied individual variables. Harold Stevenson and Robert Hess contributed much to this early phase of research. Most notably, they reported that although Asian and American mothers believe that effort is more important than ability in their children's school performance, American mothers and their children are stronger believers than their Asian counterparts in the importance of innate ability (Hess, Chih-Miei, and McDevitt, 1987; Stevenson and Lee, 1990). Stevenson and his colleagues continued investigating this cultural difference in student motivation throughout the 1990s. As we have argued elsewhere, they advanced a hypothesis that was compelling but fundamentally flawed (Bempechat and Drago-Severson, 1999).

Principally, Stevenson proposed that the higher achievement of Asian as compared to American students was the result of a culturally embedded belief in the critical role that effort plays in school achievement. In other words, Stevenson argued that Asian students were outperforming American students because they adhered to what he termed an effort model of learning. In contrast, American students were said to be doing relatively poorly because they endorsed what he termed an ability model of learning (Stevenson and Stigler, 1992). We demonstrated that none of the published work contains correlation tables that include data on effort attributions, posing a serious problem for researchers wishing to examine this major claim (Bempechat and Drago-Severson, 1999). In any case, given the correlational nature of the data, no such causal connection is possible. Furthermore, both Stevenson's work and the TIMSS investigations have found multiple instances in which American students indicate stronger beliefs in the value of effort than their Asian peers, the latter of whom have been shown to endorse, at times, stronger ability beliefs than their American peers (Beaton and others, 1996a; Stevenson, Chen, and Lee, 1993; Stevenson and Stigler, 1992; Stevenson, Lee, and Stigler, 1986).

This research put culture at the center of its investigation, but, ironically, it has not been sensitive to the ways in which students in different cultures differentially understand central concepts such as effort and ability. Instead, researchers have implicitly assumed that all students, no matter their origin, interpret these constructs in the same way—the American way. In other words, researchers have overlaid U.S. meanings onto non-U.S. students and parents.

This is problematic for two reasons. First, as Holloway (1988) has eloquently demonstrated, Japanese and Chinese parents and children view effort as multifaceted. In addition to being viewed as a critical factor in improving performance, effort is seen as a means to fulfill social obligations to one's family, peers, and community to do one's best. Effort is very much socially oriented. Second, the cross-national literature has tended to treat culture as monolithic. Although culture does indeed serve as an organizing principle for its members (Bruner, 1996; Shweder, 1990; Sinha and Sinha, 1997; Spiro, 1993), there are nonetheless individual differences in the ways in which people make meaning of achievement-related constructs. At this point in our collective knowledge, attention needs to be paid to the nature and richness of these within-culture individual differences.

Cross-National Achievement: Beyond TIMSS

With the release of each IEA-sponsored international study of achievement, the finding that tends to be of most interest to parents, educators, and policymakers is the rank ordering of nations according to outcomes. Given the nature of these international assessments, these outcomes reflect achievement in basic skills (such as computation) rather than higher-order cognitive skills involving creativity and problem solving. We have recently argued that in many respects, this information is less interesting to those concerned about improving educational practice and school performance (Bempechat, Jimenez, and Boulay, forthcoming). In fact, researchers involved in the TIMSS work have begun to question ways in which future cross-national assessments of mathematics and science achievement can be more sensitive to the influences that culture and context bring to bear on student achievement.

Hatano and Inagaki (1998) have sensitized us to the relationship between the value that a culture places on a particular academic discipline and subsequent self-construals of members of that culture and their standards of educational attainment. In this context, Bempechat, Jimenez, and Boulay (forthcoming) have argued that cross-national research on mathematics and science achievement can inform us all about the rich and varied ways that students, teachers, and parents conceptualize the meaning and value of learning. Indeed, it can help us understand the cognitive goals that each culture has for its students.

This kind of insight is critical if we are to avoid the methodological pitfalls that have dogged the TIMSS efforts. As we mentioned earlier, many educators and public policymakers have taken to overlaying findings from certain nations onto others (Reynolds and Farrell, 1996). Most common of these has been the tendency to argue that if American and English students embrace the value of effort as much as their Japanese and Singaporean peers do, their competence in mathematics and science will improve.

This may seem, at first glance, to be a reasonable interpretative approach to the growing database of international comparisons. Nevertheless, this reasoning is fundamentally flawed in its simplicity. As Elliott and his colleagues have noted (Elliott, Hufton, Illushin, and Willis, forthcoming; Chapter Four, this volume), it is not only important that effort is seen as crucial for achievement in a given domain; it is also essential that such achievement is perceived to be of sufficient importance that expending high levels of effort in pursuit of such a goal is held to be worthwhile. In their cross-cultural studies, they note that although many students emphasized the importance of working hard in order to succeed academically, such cognitions were not necessarily manifested in high levels of task engagement or work rate. To add further complexity, many of their Western informants thought that they were working hard (their judgments being largely based on adult feedback and comparison with peers in their immediate communities), yet from a comparative international perspective, this was patently not the case. Although each culture seemed to share a similar understanding of what was meant by the term *effort,* each was using a different scale to assess the extent of this; thus, the notion of "working hard" appeared to be construed very differently across cultures. The complexities involved are massive: every nation, and every community in each nation, has a geography, an economy, and prevalent work and lifestyles, practices, beliefs, and values and is influenced by the wider culture (even globally) in ways and to degrees that are integral to understanding differential achievement outcomes.

Adding yet another layer of depth, it is interesting that many American educators, surveying the TIMSS results, have embraced an implicit assumption that higher-achieving students are more likely to choose careers in science, mathematics, engineering, or technology. The national push toward higher standards through high-stakes testing and teacher accountability may indeed be one manifestation of this assumption. Instead, Rodney Cocking (personal communication, Nov. 2, 2001) and Susan Holloway (personal communication, Nov. 2, 2001) report that their Chinese and Japanese colleagues are confronting the fact that higher-achieving students are less satisfied with their mathematics learning, and many are opting out of technologically related careers. In other words, where mathematics and science are concerned, there is not necessarily a direct link between higher achievement and career choice. In contrast, American students, while lower achieving than their Japanese and Chinese peers, report greater enjoyment and satisfaction with their learning. It may indeed be these lower-achieving but more motivated students who choose technologically related courses of study and careers.

Indeed, the issues we face are larger and more complex than, say, raising standards in order to raise achievement. What if, in the process of raising standards, many of our students begin to lose confidence in their abilities to learn mathematics and science? The work of Covington (1992, 1996, 1998), in particular, has shown how increasing academic competitiveness and pressure in the hope of raising standards can lead some students to disengage and disrupt as a means to hide concerns about their ability, and thus protect their sense of self-worth. Another strategy for such students is to select tasks and disciplines where demands are low and any risk of failure is minimized. Such unintended consequences have the potential to negatively affect the numbers of students choosing academically demanding classes in high school, thereby affecting the number of students choosing majors in the most challenging disciplines in college, and thus in their future careers. If some threshold of raising standards results in declining confidence, what will we have accomplished?

The work of the chapter authors is designed to avoid simplistic prescriptions. Their research is situated in China, England, Russia, Japan, and the United States and is focused on uncovering indigenous concepts that organize and guide individuals' orientation toward learning and achievement. For example, Li's studies of Chinese conceptions of learning have revealed many native concepts that have not emerged through traditional cross-cultural surveys and really cannot do so. Specifically, she found that among adults, learning means humility, self-perfection, moral striving, contributing to society, and having the "heart and mind for wanting to learn" (Li, 2001a, forthcoming).

In Japan, for example, mothers and their children tend to place more emphasis than do their American counterparts on effort as a cause of low achievement in mathematics, but their relative weighting of effort appears unrelated to the students' grades in school (Holloway, Kashiwagi, Hess, and Azuma, 1986). Elliott and his colleagues found that understanding the complexities behind these and several other such puzzles could best be achieved by combining classroom observations, in-depth interviews, and an analysis of the broader sociocultural context (Elliot, Hufton, Illushin, and Willis, 2001; Elliott, Hufton, Hildreth, and Illushin, 1999; Elliott, Hufton, Illushin, and Lauchlan, 2001; Hufton, Elliott, and Illushin, 2002; Hufton and Elliott, 2000; Chapter Four, this volume).

Cross-National Achievement in the Context of Educational Reform

Each of the nations in which the authors in this volume have been working is living through a period of educational soul searching. Each nation is trying in different ways to reform education so as to improve motivation. In order to deepen our understanding of the meaning of cross-national differences in achievement, we need to understand the goals that different nations have for the education of children and youth and the means by which they believe they can achieve these goals. In the United States, for example, persistent underachievement has gradually led to an increase in high-stakes testing and accountability. In Massachusetts, for example, the Massachusetts Comprehensive Assessment System (MCAS), a statewide testing initiative, has generated intensive debates about the state's pedagogical goals. Opponents decry what has come to be termed a "one-size-fits-all" assessment system, as well as teachers' somewhat natural tendencies to teach to the test. Proponents argue that minimal standards of competency are a prerequisite to graduating students who are prepared for the workforce. Against this backdrop of public discourse is the fact that the sophomore cohort of the 2000–2001 academic year is the first that will be required to have a passing grade on the MCAS in order to receive their high school diplomas. Students who fail the test as sophomores have four more chances to pass it before the end of their senior years.

As of March 2002, 75 percent of high school juniors had passed the mathematics portion of the test, and 82 percent had passed the English portion ("On the MCAS Track," 2002), and they have three chances to retake the exam before their expected graduation in 2003. However, the Massachusetts Commissioner of Education, David Driscoll, has estimated that 10–15 percent of students remain at risk for failing. This number could be as high as 20–30 percent in poor urban areas. Despite the fact that 67 percent of students report that the need to pass the test has motivated them to work harder, approximately 54 percent of students recently polled stated that they are not taking advantage of tutorial sessions even though they have already failed the exam (Mass Insight Education, 2002).

In England, recent government education reforms (also involving an accountability model based on high-stakes testing) and a raft of inner-city initiatives have sought to raise educational standards, yet it is unclear to what extent these can prove effective where the value of schooling is not perceived by students living in economically disadvantaged communities. The shift toward increased central control has resulted in the imposition of a particularly draconian, centrally imposed curriculum and pedagogy that has reduced teachers' ability to respond to their perceptions of student needs or interests. Such a trend runs counter to the U.S. achievement motivation literature that stresses the importance of authenticity, student choice, and control (Seifert and O'Keefe, 2001; Yair, 2000). However, while many elements of U.S. and U.K. cultures have much in common, it is important to recognize that the strong American emphasis on individual autonomy underpinning many education reform initiatives (Sizer, 1992) may not necessarily be applicable to the U.K. context.

Although conceptions of learning in China are particularly different from those in the West, there is increasing debate over instituting major changes in the national curriculum. Since the open door policy in the early 1980s, China has been struggling with its educational system. The mismatch between the deeply entrenched school system that is mostly geared toward examination and the growing demand on learners' achieving more adaptive abilities and new levels of skills has prompted nationwide educational reform. Instead of adhering to traditional pedagogy, such as rote memorization and teacher-centered classroom instructions, educators are now seeking ways to promote deeper understanding of subjects, critical thinking skills, and creativity in children. To institute change, interestingly, Western educational theories and practices have often been sought as a source of inspiration and a model for scientific innovations and economic success. It is therefore a particularly significant historical moment to examine how the deep-seated Chinese cultural notions of learning and achievement face challenges and transformations in this process of large-scale change.

In Russia, the rapidly changing economy is challenging long-held beliefs about the inherent value of becoming a highly educated individual. Despite the long-standing strength of mathematics and science (Bucur and Eklof, 1999), much value was also placed on being a person of culture, well versed in literature, languages, art, and the wider humanities. More recently, it would appear that concerns are becoming widespread about a loss of student values, particularly in relation to school (Popovand and Kondrat'eva, 2000). Furthermore, some subjects are now being valued primarily in economic terms, and older students, certainly those at universities, are increasingly motivated to study those subjects that offer the greatest financial rewards (Rutkevich, 1999). Given that students' motivation may vary substantially from one subject to another (Mischel and Peake, 1982), the Russian context is likely to provide valuable insights into the relationship between rapid economic transformation and motivation regarding different academic disciplines. However, here also it is necessary to recognize a distinct historical and cultural legacy very different from that of the West that should make us pause before offering generic solutions to national problems. The belief on the part of many Russians that the introduction of Western educational models and practices would help raise performance has declined in striking parallel with disenchantment about other Western influences, both cultural and economic. As Alexander (2000, p. 100) notes, official reports on Russian education by Western agencies such as the World Bank (in 1996) and the Organization for Economic Co-operation and Development reflect an ethnocentric belief that a pedagogy underpinned by a more individualistic orientation should replace classroom practices perceived to be old-fashioned. Alexander argues that in neglecting Russia's historical and cultural traditions and its long-standing educational achievements, such recommendations are both superficial and naive.

In Japan, youth can be assessed favorably relative to students in Western countries on almost any indicator of adjustment or achievement, including suicide, drug use, depression, violence, and teenage pregnancy (Holloway, 2000). The general health and well-being of Japanese youth have prompted outside observers to conclude that Japanese schools are functioning well. Indeed, many strong points can be identified in an examination of the Japanese educational system. The status and work conditions of teachers are favorable (Tominaga, 1979). Beginning teachers are paid at a level equivalent to similarly educated peers in other fields and receive annual increments until retirement age (Okano and Tsuchiya, 1999). Informal training opportunities, such as school workshops and voluntary study groups, are widely available (Kinney, 1998; Sato, 1992), and more recently, formal opportunities to visit other schools, educational institutions, and research centers have been created for novice and experienced teachers (Sato, 1992).

A substantial number of reforms implemented over the past decade stem from strong concerns expressed within the country (Horio and Sabouret, 1990). At the classroom level, issues of concern include increases in bullying, school refusal, and openly resistant students (Nakane, 1990). In Ministry of Education reports, students are frequently characterized as parochial rather than globally oriented, overly busy and competitive, lacking in social skills, and insufficiently independent (Okano and Tsuchiya, 1999). Numerous remedies for these problems have been implemented, including individualizing instruction, reducing the number of hours of school per week, increasing the opportunity to take electives, mandating teacher training courses in student guidance, and increasing the socialization role of institutions outside the school. In addition, economic and structural changes are gaining the attention of the Ministry of Education; one major issue has been the increased need for highly skilled upper-level managers of large international corporations. Reforms addressing these new market demands include developing a multitrack system featuring elite six-year secondary schools focused on science and technology (Okano and Tsuchiya, 1999).

Students' views of learning and motivation to achieve are likely to be significantly affected by these attempts to individualize instruction, provide choices, lessen competition, and open up more free time, all of which are consistent with fostering self-directed learning according to current theory generated in Western countries. Of significant interest, however, is how these techniques will be appropriated within a cultural milieu that has traditionally emphasized alternative methods of learning and motivation.

One can readily see that international comparisons of achievement, with their focus on surveys of students' achievement-related beliefs, can offer only limited information that can be of practical use to teachers and policymakers. We stand to learn much more, and thus have more to offer educators, if we move research in a new direction, one that poses contextualized research questions, pays careful attention to cultural nuances in learning and motivation, and considers the ways in which individuals within cultures may share overarching cultural views but conceptualize them in very different ways (see Markus, Mullally, and Kitayama, 1997).

New Directions for Research

Researchers can take meaningful steps to move the field forward. Chief among these are contextualizing research questions, developing authentic means of inquiry, and acknowledging within-group differences.

Contextualizing Research Questions. Rather than assessing achievement-related beliefs in a decontextualized fashion, as has been done in previous cross-national investigations, it is important that we examine the ways in which orientations toward school and learning exist within the social and cultural structures—particularly the school and family—that form students' "ecological niche" (Harkness and Super, 1992). Researchers should expect to find some commonality within a nation due to common social structures and foundational schema relevant to that society, for example, an orientation toward self-improvement in Japan (see Markus, Mullally, and Kitayama, 1997). However, we believe that investigators also should expect to find intranational variation among youth.

From a methodological perspective, the great value in cultural studies lies in deepening our understanding of the social, cultural, political, and historical contexts that drive nations' pedagogical goals, practices, and reforms. One important means of accomplishing this is by focusing on how parents, teachers, and students in different sociocultural contexts describe their schools and their educational and teaching experiences. Attempts to draw out meaning making in cultural context will provide us with a sense of how individuals construct their own emic, or idiosyncratic, understandings of the purposes of learning and schooling in their own societies.

In this regard, in-depth qualitative inquiry can provide the rich and contextualized information that we need in order to understand the meanings of particular educational beliefs and attitudes in cultural context, defined by criteria from within the culture in question (Schurmans and Dasen, 1992). At the same time, quantitative data derived from questionnaires and surveys of students' schooling experiences may also contribute to understandings. Thus, while the qualitative research may offer unique insights into individual meaning making, quantitative measures can serve to ground new research in existing theory (see Shweder, 1997).

Developing Authentic Means of Inquiry. Cross-national and cross-ethnic surveys of achievement motivation have relied almost exclusively on the language and constructs of the research literature. By definition, children's responses to forced-choice or Likert-type scales are constrained by the constructs that researchers deem, a priori, to be important organizing principles in children's thinking about school achievement. This strategy is an etic one, in the sense that these constructs are imposed on children rather than derived from their own expressions of understanding (see Bempechat and Drago-Severson, 1999).

What we have, then, is a body of literature in which, on the basis of their answers to questionnaire items, students become classified along abstract categories. Even more worrisome is that these students may all too easily become identified as synonymous with dichotomous variables. For example, there are students who are either entity or incremental theorists (Bempechat, London, and Dweck, 1991; Dweck, 1999). This means they believe that intelligence, respectively, is either limited or limitless. In addition, there are students who are either ego involved or task involved in their learning (Nicholls, 1984; Nicholls, Cheung, Lauer, and Patachnick, 1989). This means, respectively, that they are primarily concerned with either looking smart relative to others or improving their own performance, regardless of that of others in their classroom.

No one who has conducted work of this nature has ever argued that children think about school achievement in one of two ways. Yet by its very nature, this kind of research is incapable of revealing the rich and varied ways in which students understand and speak about central achievement-related beliefs, such as effort, ability, and intelligence. Students' own perspectives—their personal emic views—are virtually absent from the scholarly discourse. As we have argued elsewhere (Bempechat, Jimenez, and Boulay, forthcoming), it is remarkable that so many researchers (including one of this chapter's authors) have conducted so much research on children's achievement beliefs without ever having had a conversation with a child. Despite this, many of us have made claims in the literature about implications for practice, based on which puzzle a child may have chosen to work on following a failure experience or which question stem out of a choice of five that a child might have circled.

If we were to sit down with a ninth grader, for example, and ask her to talk about what she thinks about mastering English and how she learns, she would never say, "I am an entity theorist." However, as Quihuis, Bempechat, Jimenez, and Boulay demonstrate in Chapter Five, she might very well express a view such as Dulce's, a fifteen year old who explained to us, "Right now, I don't speak it [English], but if I spoke it well, if I practiced every day, it would change. There is no limit [to how much English you can learn] I think you can learn it all, every day you can learn a new word. I understand [English], but don't like it because I don't practice it." Dulce's understanding is complex and defies easy categorization. She could be labeled an incremental theorist because she states clearly that "there is no limit" to learning. However, this would not take into account the fact that, for her, liking a subject is an important determinant of the amount of effort she invests in learning.

Abel's understanding is even more complex than his classmate Dulce's. Some of his statements indicate entity beliefs; others indicate incremental beliefs:

> Depends on where you come [from], because I know people who only speak Spanish and have many problems with English, in writing, reading, speaking it, but if you have always studied English, you won't have problems if you learned it at a young age. But if you come from another country, you will have trouble, but if you practice you may be able to overcome. But there are people who can't. They speak it, but with an accent. Some people just can't continue. English is very difficult and you need to start it from small, I mean like the accent that won't go away.

These brief excerpts from interviews show how rich and varied are the beliefs that students hold. Similarly, none of the Chinese conceptions of intelligence revealed by Li's research (2001a), such as humility and self-perfection, can be accommodated by Dweck's framework. In our research and in the work presented in this volume, we aim to capture this kind of meaningful variation in students' understandings. When we urge more authentic means of inquiry, we are referring not only to qualitative interviews, but also to observational studies of students' learning and focus group discussion, to name but a few examples of the kinds of research likely to yield insights into the motivational underpinnings of success and failure.

Acknowledging Within-Group Differences. In the 1980s, when cross-national research began to reveal that Japanese and Chinese students were significantly outperforming their American peers, the national discourse focused on how the American educational system could be reformed to put its students on par with the best students in other countries. While some may not have realized it, everyone was speaking, of course, about average mathematics scores. In other words, the average Japanese and Chinese mathematics score was significantly higher than the average American score. The fact that there existed lower-achieving Japanese students and higher-achieving American students was lost in the debate.

When time and further investigations repeatedly replicated these between-country differences, educators and scholars began turning their attention to within-country differences. What are the characteristics of lower-achieving students in a nation where average achievement is relatively high? And what are the characteristics of higher-achieving students in a nation where average achievement is relatively low? Some researchers in the United States have examined this issue in the context of ethnic minority achievement (see Bempechat, 1998; Boardman, Harrington, and Horowitz, 1987; Fordham, 1986). Understanding school success in students ordinarily considered to be at risk for school failure may hold insights into helping all students achieve their intellectual potential.

It is important to note that our collective research (Bempechat, Jimenez, and Graham, 1997; Elliott, Hufton, Hildreth, and Illushin, 1999; Elliott, Hufton, Illushin, and Willis, 2001; Holloway, 2000; Hufton, Elliott, and Illushin, 2002; Li, Yue, and Yuan, 2001; Li, 2001b), as well as that of colleagues in the field, has shown that constructs that seem to explain national or ethnic differences in achievement do not always do well at predicting within-country (or within-ethnic-group) achievement (Shen and Pedulla, 2000; Steinberg, Dornbusch, and Brown, 1992). We know that children from the same social circumstances have been shown to differ in their aspirations and achievement. For example, Li's recent work on the individual and social self in learning among Chinese adolescents demonstrated that girls and low-income children expressed consistently more learning and achievement goals and beliefs than did boys and higher-income peers. Thus, in keeping with current theorizing in psychological anthropology, cultural psychology, and achievement motivation, our conceptual model views achievement beliefs as socially constructed (Bruner, 1990; Strauss, 1999; Strauss, Ravid, Zelcer, and Berliner, 1999). In other words, in order to understand variation within and between cultures, the research community needs to place more value on emic research.

The Promise of Emic Research

In their detailed review of the literature on motivation related to academic achievement, Murphy and Alexander (2000) note that most of the work was undertaken by American researchers studying American students and that nearly all was of a Western philosophical orientation. As a result, they questioned whether the conclusions and implications that result can be generalized to other cultures. However, with respect to their call for cross-cultural studies, they make no reference to methodological complexities, appearing not to find difficulties with extending traditional, quantitative approaches across cultures. Thus, their suggestion appears to be for the continuation of traditional methodologies to examine whether findings pertaining to the United States are replicated in other cultures. Furthermore, by suggesting such research questions as, "Are successful students in other cultures also those who are mastery oriented and intrinsically motivated?" (p. 45), they appear to demonstrate few misgivings about employing Western, etic constructs in cultures where they may have little meaning or substance. We endorse Murphy and Alexander's call for cross-cultural research, but we contend that we should recognize that for the examination of other cultures, Western findings may fail to apply and, more fundamental, the constructs and methodologies that often underpin them may actually be inappropriate.

Shweder (1997) has described ethnographic research as a "process of discovery." For those of us who have been trained in traditional quantitative methods of inquiry, qualitative research can seem formidable indeed. Interviews do not yield findings that differ on a categorical scale. There is no doubt, however, that we can move our field and our understandings forward if we embrace methods that cultural psychologists and cognitive anthropologists have employed for a long time (LeVine, 1997; LeVine, Miller, and West, 1988). When we allow students, parents, and teachers to speak for themselves, using carefully crafted interviews that allow participants to take discussions wherever they wish them to go, we open ourselves up to insights that have not been able to emerge in research based on prior theory and findings (Elliott, Hufton, Anderman, and Illushin, 2000).

A key aspect of ethnography is observation. Without this element as a cornerstone of comparative studies, detailed, richly textured interviews are likely to provide only a limited picture of the factors that lead students to be academically motivated and engaged. In the comparative studies of Elliott and his colleagues, for example, observation of international differences in teacher and student classroom behavior raised many issues that were profitably explored by means of follow-up interviews. For example, teachers in Russia and the United States highlighted the importance of praise, yet it was only by means of classroom observations that the radically different nature and frequency of teacher affirmation in each culture could be discerned and subsequently discussed (Elliott, Hufton, Illushin, and Willis, forthcoming). Similarly, observation of actual student behavior in class highlighted a widespread discrepancy between student statements and actual behavior in the

U.S. context and thus helped the team to recognize differences in student understandings about what was meant by "working hard." However, interviews (individually or in groups), like surveys, may fail to reveal the influence of social processes in motivation. Certainly, an increasing number of motivation theorists have come to believe that social factors have often been underestimated (Schunk, 2000; Murphy and Alexander, 2000). In referring to social factors here, we are not talking merely of the social goals (Miller and others, 1996; Wentzel, 1991) that students may be able to discuss in interviews and are of interest to an increasing number of researchers, but also the operation and influence of subtle social forces that students may fail to recognize or prefer to deemphasize. Although attempts have been made to study these influences (Ryan, 2001), they have tended to rely heavily on traditional approaches that use sociometry and surveys. As a result, the distinction between student perceptions of peer influences and actuality may be confounded.

As we and others have argued, calls for authenticity and contextualization do not imply that researchers should abandon quantitative methods of inquiry (Bempechat, Jimenez, and Boulay, forthcoming; Bruner, 1990; Lawrence-Lightfoot and Davis, 1997). Rather, we believe that comprehensive research should be of a hybrid and cyclical nature. For example, insights that flow from interviews and field studies may form a basis for follow-up questionnaires in which some, but not necessarily all, items are studied in each culture. The results of quantitative studies may help in two ways: permitting generalization to larger samples and informing the design of further stages of data gathering. In calling for cross-cultural research on motivation to embrace a combination of methodologies that tease out cultural and contextual differences in thinking and understanding, we do, however, argue against the exclusive adoption of the current dominant paradigm in psychology: "There is no *one* royal road to truth in the social sciences . . . All methods have their strengths and weaknesses and all are, in varying degrees, messy and unsatisfactory because life is messy and unsatisfactory" (Coffield, Robinson, and Sarsby, 1980, p. 16).

References

Alexander, R. J. *Culture and Pedagogy: International Comparisons in Primary Education.* Cambridge, Mass.: Blackwell, 2000.

Ames, C., and Archer, J. "Mothers' Beliefs About the Role of Ability and Effort in School Learning." *Journal of Educational Psychology,* 1987, 71, 409–414.

Ames, R., and Ames, C. (eds.). *Student Motivation.* Orlando, Fla.: Academic Press, 1984.

Beaton, A. E., and others. *Mathematics Achievement in the Middle School Years: IEA's Third International Mathematics and Science Study (TIMSS).* Boston: Center for the Study of Testing, Evaluation, and Educational Policy, Boston College, 1996a.

Beaton, A. E., and others. *Science Achievement in the Middle School Years: IEA's Third International Mathematics and Science Study (TIMSS).* Boston: Center for the Study of Testing, Evaluation, and Educational Policy, Boston College, 1996b.

Bempechat, J. *Against the Odds: How "At Risk" Students Exceed Expectations.* San Francisco: Jossey-Bass, 1998.

Bempechat, J., and Drago-Severson, E. "Cross-National Differences in Academic Achievement: Beyond Etic Conceptions of Children's Understandings." *Review of Educational Research*, 1999, *69*, 287–314.

Bempechat, J., Jimenez, N., and Boulay, B. "Cultural-Cognitive Issues in Academic Achievement: New Directions for Cross-National Research." In A. C. Porter and A. Gamoran (eds.), *Methodological Advances in Cross-National Surveys of Educational Achievement*. Washington, D.C.: National Academy Press, forthcoming.

Bempechat, J., Jimenez, N., and Graham, S. "Motivational Factors in Learning: Implications for Poor and Minority Children and Youth." *Journal of Child and Youth Care Work*, 1997, *11*, 48–60.

Bempechat, J., London, P., and Dweck, C. S. "Children's Conceptions of Ability in Major Domains: An Interview and Experimental Study." *Child Study Journal*, 1991, *21*, 11–35.

Bempechat, J., Nakkula, M., Wu, J., and Ginsburg, H. "Attributions as Predictors of Math Achievement: A Comparative Study." *Journal of Research and Development in Education*, 1996, *29*, 53–59.

Boardman, S., Harrington, C., and Horowitz, S. "Successful Woman: A Psychological Investigation of Family, Class and Education." In B. Gutek and L. Larwood (eds.), *Women's Career Development*. Thousand Oaks, Calif.: Sage, 1987.

Bruner, J. *Acts of Meaning*. Cambridge, Mass.: Harvard University Press, 1990.

Bruner, J. *The Culture of Education*. Cambridge, Mass.: Harvard University Press, 1996.

Bucur, M., and Eklof, B. "Russia and Eastern Europe." In R. F. Arnove and C. A. Torres (eds.), *Comparative Education: The Dialectic of the Global and the Local*. Lanham, Md.: Rowman & Littlefield, 1999.

Coffield, F., Robinson, P., and Sarsby, J. *A Cycle of Deprivation?* London: Heinemann, 1980.

Covington, M. V. *Making the Grade: A Self-Worth Perspective on Motivation and School Reform*. Cambridge, Mass.: Harvard University Press, 1992.

Covington, M. V. "The Myth of Intensification." *Educational Researcher*, 1996, *25*(8), 22–27.

Covington, M. V. *The Will to Learn: A Guide to Motivating Young People*. Cambridge, England: Cambridge University Press, 1998.

Dweck, C. S. "The Role of Expectations and Attributions in the Alleviation of Learned Helplessness." *Journal of Personality and Social Psychology*, 1975, *31*, 674–685.

Dweck, C. S. *Self-Theories: Their Role in Motivation, Personality and Development*. New York: Psychology Press, 1999.

Eccles, J. "School and Family Effects on the Ontogeny of Children's Interests, Self-Perceptions, and Activity Choices." In J. Jacobs (ed.), *Nebraska Symposium on Motivation: Developmental Perspectives on Motivation*. Vol. 40. Lincoln: University of Nebraska Press, 1993.

Eccles (Parsons), J., Adler, T., and Meece, J. "Sex Differences in Achievement: A Test of Alternative Theories." *Journal of Personality and Social Psychology*, 1984, *46*, 26–43.

Eccles, J., and Wigfield, A. "In the Mind of the Actor: The Structure of Adolescents' Achievement Task Values and Expectancy-Related Beliefs." *Personality and Social Psychology Bulletin*, 1995, *21*, 215–225.

Elliott, J., Hufton, N., Anderman, E., and Illushin, L. "The Psychology of Motivation and Its Relevance to Educational Practice." *Educational and Child Psychology*, 2000, *17*, 122–138.

Elliott, J. G., Hufton, N. R., Hildreth, A., and Illushin, L. "Factors Influencing Educational Motivation: A Study of Attitudes, Expectations and Behaviour of Children in Sunderland, Kentucky, and St. Petersburg." *British Educational Research Journal*, 1999, *25*, 75–94.

Elliott, J. G., Hufton, N. R., Illushin, L., and Lauchlan, F. "Motivation in the Junior Years: International Perspectives on Children's Attitudes, Expectations and Behaviour and Their Relationship to Educational Achievement." *Oxford Review of Education*, 2001, *27*, 37–68.

Elliott, J. G., Hufton, N., Illushin, L., and Willis, W. " 'The Kids Are Doing All Right': Differences in Parental Satisfaction, Expectation and Attribution in St. Petersburg, Sunderland and Kentucky." *Cambridge Journal of Education,* 2001, *31,* 179–204.

Elliott, J., Hufton, N., Illushin, L., and Willis, W. *Performance in Context: Motivation and Achievement from an International Perspective.* New York: Palgrave Press, forthcoming.

Fordham, S. *Blacked Out: Dilemmas of Race, Identity, and Success at Capital High.* Chicago: University of Chicago Press, 1986.

Ginsburg, H. "Mathematics Learning Disabilities: A View from Developmental Psychology." *Journal of Learning Disabilities,* 1997, *30,* 20–33.

Harkness, S., and Super, C. "Parental Ethnotheories in Action." In I. E. Sigel, A. V. McGillicuddy-DeLisi, and J. J. Goodnow (eds.), *Parental Belief Systems: The Psychological Consequences for Children.* (2nd ed.) Mahwah, N.J.: Erlbaum, 1992.

Harter, C., and Connell, J. "A Model of the Relationships Among Children's Academic Achievement and Their Self-Perceptions of Competence, Control, and Motivational Orientation." In J. Nicholls (ed.), *Advances in Motivation and Achievement: The Development of Achievement Motivation.* Vol. 3. Greenwich, Conn.: JAI Press, 1984.

Hatano, G., and Inagaki, K. "Cultural Contexts of Schooling Revisited: A Review of 'The Learning Gap' from a Cultural Psychology Perspective." In S. G. Paris and H. M. Wellman (eds.), *Global Prospects for Education: Development, Culture and Schooling.* Washington, D.C.: American Psychological Association, 1998.

Hess, R. D., Chih-Miei, C., and McDevitt, T. M. "Cultural Variations in Family Beliefs About Children's Performance in Mathematics: Comparisons Among People's Republic of China, Chinese-American, and Caucasian-American Families." *Journal of Educational Psychology,* 1987, *79,* 179–188.

Holloway, S. "Concepts of Ability and Effort in Japan and the United States." *Review of Educational Research,* 1988, *58,* 327–345.

Holloway, S. D. *Contested Childhood: Diversity and Change in Japanese Preschools.* New York: Routledge, 2000.

Holloway, S. D., Kashiwagi, K., Hess, R. D., and Azuma, H. "Causal Attributions by Japanese and American Mothers About Performance in Mathematics." *International Journal of Psychology,* 1986, *21,* 269–286.

Horio, T., and Sabouret, J. "Education in Japan: The Issues at Stake at the Dawn of the Twenty-First Century." In C. Chiland and J. G. Young (eds.), *Why Children Reject School: Views from Seven Countries.* New Haven, Conn.: Yale University Press, 1990.

Hufton, N. R., and Elliott, J. G. "Motivation to Learn: The Pedagogical Nexus in the Russian School: Some Implications for Transnational Research and Policy Borrowing." *Educational Studies,* 2000, *26,* 115–136.

Hufton, N., Elliott, J. G., and Illushin, L. "Educational Motivation and Engagement: Qualitative Accounts from Three Countries." *British Educational Research Journal,* 2002, *28*(2), 265–289.

Kinney, C. *Teachers and the Teaching Profession in Japan.* Washington, D.C.: National Institute on Student Achievement, Curriculum, and Assessment, Office of Educational Research and Improvement, U.S. Department of Education, 1998.

Lawrence-Lightfoot, S., and Davis, J. H. *The Art and Science of Portraiture.* San Francisco: Jossey-Bass, 1997.

LeVine, R. "Child Rearing as Cultural Adaptation." In P. Leiderman, S. Tulkin, and A. Rosenfeld (eds.), *Culture and Infancy: Variations in the Human Experience.* Orlando, Fla.: Academic Press, 1997.

LeVine, R., Miller, P., and West, M. (eds.). *Parental Behavior in Diverse Societies.* New Directions for Child Development, no. 40. San Francisco: Jossey-Bass, 1988.

Li, J. "Chinese Conceptualization of Learning." *Ethos,* 2001a, *29,* 1–28.

Li, J. "Conceptions of Knowledge and Learning Among U.S. and Chinese Preschoolers." Paper presented at the biennial meetings of the Society for Research in Child Development, Minneapolis, Minn., Apr. 2001b.

Li, J. "High Abilities and Excellence: A Cultural Perspective." In L. V. Shavinina and M. Ferrari (eds.), *Beyond Knowledge: Extracognitive Facets in Developing High Ability*. Mahwah, N.J.: Erlbaum, forthcoming.

Li, J., Yue, X.-D., and Yuan, S. "Individual Self and Social Self in Learning Among Chinese Adolescents." Paper presented at the biennial meetings of the Society for Research in Child Development, Minneapolis, Minn., Apr. 21, 2001.

Markus, H. R., Mullally, P. R., and Kitayama, S. "Selfways: Diversity in Modes of Cultural Participation." In U. Neisser and D. A. Jopling (eds.), *The Conceptual Self in Context: Culture, Experience, Self-Understanding*. Cambridge, England: Cambridge University Press, 1997.

Marsh, H. "Relations Among Dimensions of Self-Attribution, Dimensions of Self-Concept, and Academic Achievement." *Journal of Educational Psychology*, 1984, *76*, 1291–1308.

Marsh, H. W., and Yeung, A. S. "Causal Effects of Academic Self-Concept on Academic Achievement: Structural Equation Models of Longitudinal Data." *Journal of Educational Psychology*, 1997, *89*(1), 41–54.

Marsh, H., and others. "The Relationship Between Dimensions of Self-Attribution and Dimensions of Self-Concept." *Journal of Educational Psychology*, 1984, *76*, 3–32.

Martin, M. O., and others. *1999: International Science Report*. Boston: International Study Center, Boston College, 2000.

Mass Insight Education. "Taking Charge: Urban High School Students Speak Out About MCAS, Academics, and Extra Help Programs." Boston: Mass Insight Education, Mar. 2002. (Report.)

Miller, R. B., and others. "Engagement in Academic Work: The Role of Learning Goals, Future Consequences, Pleasing Others and Perceived Ability." *Contemporary Educational Psychology*, 1996, *21*, 388–422.

Mischel, W., and Peake, P. K. "Beyond Déjà Vu in the Search for Cross-Situational Consistency." *Psychological Review*, 1982, *89*, 730–755.

Mullis, I. V., and others. *TIMSS 1999: International Mathematics Report*. Boston: International Study Center, Boston College, 2000.

Murphy, P. K., and Alexander, P. A. "A Motivated Exploration of Motivation Terminology." *Contemporary Educational Psychology*, 2000, *25*, 3–53.

Nakane, A. "School Refusal: Psychopathology and Natural History." In C. Chiland and J. G. Young (eds.), *Why Children Reject School: Views from Seven Countries*. New Haven, Conn.: Yale University Press, 1990.

Nicholls, J. G. "Conceptions of Ability and Achievement Motivation." In R. E. Ames and C. Ames (eds.), *Research on Motivation in Education*, Vol. 1: *Student Motivation*. New York: Harcourt, 1984.

Nicholls, J. G., Cheung, P. C., Lauer, J., and Patachnick, M. "Individual Differences in Academic Motivation: Perceived Ability, Goals, Beliefs, and Values." *Learning and Individual Differences*, 1989, *1*, 63–84.

Okano, K., and Tsuchiya, M. *Education in Contemporary Japan: Inequality and Diversity*. Cambridge, England: Cambridge University Press, 1999.

"On the MCAS Track." *Boston Globe*, Mar. 22, 2002. (Editorial.)

Popovand, V. A., and Kondrat'eva, O. I. "Change in the Motivational-Value Orientations of Young People in School." *Russian Education and Society*, 2000, *42*, 77–85.

Reynolds, D., and Farrell, S. *Worlds Apart? A Review of International Surveys of Educational Achievement Involving England*. London: Her Majesty's Stationery Office, 1996.

Rutkevich, M. "Change in the Social Role of the General Education School in Russia." *Narodnoe obrazovanie*, 1999, *1–2*, 55–63.

Ryan, A. "The Peer Group as a Context for the Development of Young Adolescent Motivation and Achievement." *Child Development*, 2001, *72*, 1135–1150.

Sato, M. "Japan." In H. Leavitt (ed.), *Issues and Problems of Teacher Education: An International Handbook*. Westport, Conn.: Greenwood Press, 1992.

Schunk, D. H. "Coming to Terms with Motivation Constructs." *Contemporary Educational Psychology,* 2000, *25,* 116–119.

Schurmans, M., and Dasen, P. "Social Representations of Intelligence: Cote d'Ivoire and Switzerland." In M. V. Cranach, W. Doise, and G. Mugny (eds.), *Social Representations and the Social Bases of Knowledge.* Lewiston, N.Y.: Hogrefe & Huber, 1992.

Seifert, T. L., and O'Keefe, B. A. "The Relationship of Work Avoidance and Learning Goals to Perceived Competence, Externality and Meaning." *British Journal of Educational Psychology,* 2001, *71,* 81–92.

Shen, C., and Pedulla, J. J. "The Relationship Between Students' Achievement and Their Self-Perception of Competence and Rigour of Mathematics and Science: A Cross-National Analysis." *Assessment in Education,* 2000, *7,* 237–253.

Shweder, R. "Cultural Psychology—What Is It?" In J. Stigler, R. Shweder, and G. Herdt (eds.), *Cultural Psychology: Essays on Comparative Human Development.* Cambridge, England: Cambridge University Press, 1990.

Shweder, R. "The Surprise of Ethnography." *Ethos,* 1997, *25,* 152–163.

Sinha, D., and Sinha, M. "Orientations to Psychology: Asian and Western." In H. Kao and D. Sinha (eds.), *Asian Perspectives on Psychology.* Vol. 19. Thousand Oaks, Calif.: Sage, 1997.

Sizer, T. R. *Horace's School: Redesigning the American High School.* Boston: Houghton Mifflin, 1992.

Slavin, R. E. "Synthesis of Research on Cooperative Learning." *Educational Leadership,* 1991, *1,* 71–77.

Spiro, M. "Is the Western Conception of the Self 'Peculiar' Within the Contexts of World Cultures?" *Ethos,* 1993, *21,* 107–153.

Steinberg, L., Dornbusch, S., and Brown, B. "Ethnic Differences in Adolescent Achievement: An Ecological Perspective." *American Psychologist,* 1992, *47,* 723–729.

Stevenson, H., Chen, C., and Lee, S. "Mathematics Achievement of Chinese, Japanese, and American Children: Ten Years Later." *Science,* 1993, *259,* 53–58.

Stevenson, H. W., and Lee, S. Y. "Contexts of Achievement: A Study of American, Chinese, and Japanese Children." *Monographs of the Society for Research in Child Development,* 1990, *55*(1–2). Serial no. 221.

Stevenson, H. W., Lee, S., and Stigler, J. W. "Mathematics Achievement of Chinese, Japanese and American Children." *Science,* 1986, *231,* 693–699.

Stevenson, H. W., and Stigler, J. W. *The Learning Gap: Why Our Schools Are Failing and What We Can Learn from Japanese and Chinese Education.* New York: Simon & Schuster, 1992.

Stipek, D., and Hoffman, J. "Development of Children's Performance-Related Judgments." *Child Development,* 1980, *51,* 912–914.

Strauss, C. "The Cultural Concept and the Individualism/Collectivism Debate: Dominant and Alternative Attributions for Class in the United States." In L. Nucci, G. B. Saxe, and E. Turiel (eds.), *Culture, Thought and Development.* Mahwah, N.J.: Erlbaum, 1999.

Strauss, S., Ravid, D., Zelcer, H., and Berliner, D. C. "Teachers' Subject Matter Knowledge and Their Belief Systems About Children's Learning." In T. Nunes (ed.), *Learning to Read: An Integrated View from Research and Practice.* Norwood, Mass.: Kluwer, 1999.

Tominaga, K. (ed.). *Nihon no kaisou kouzou* [Social structure in Japan]. Tokyo: Tokyo University Press, 1979.

Weiner, B. (ed.). *Theories of Motivation: From Mechanism to Cognition.* Chicago: Markham, 1972.

Weiner, B. "The Emotional Consequences of Causal Ascriptions." In M. S. Clark and S. T. Fiske (eds.), *Affect and Cognition: The Seventeenth Annual Carnegie Symposium on Cognition.* Mahwah, N.J.: Erlbaum, 1982.

Weiner, B. "Integrating Social and Personal Theories of Achievement Strivings." *Review of Educational Research,* 1994, *64,* 557–573.

Weiner, B., Graham, S., Stern, P., and Lawson, M. E. "Using Affective Cues to Infer Causal Thoughts." *Developmental Psychology*, 1982, *18*, 278–286.

Weiner, B., Russell, D., and Lerman, D. "The Cognition-Emotion Process in Achievement-Related Contexts." *Journal of Personality and Social Psychology*, 1979, *37*, 1211–1220.

Wentzel, K. R. "Social and Academic Goals at School: Achievement Motivation in Context." In M. L. Maehr and P. R. Pintrich (eds.), *Advances in Motivation and Achievement*. Vol. 7. Greenwich, Conn.: JAI Press, 1991.

Wolleat, P., Pedro, J., Becker, A., and Fennema, E. "Sex Differences in High School Students' Causal Attributions of Performance in Mathematics." *Journal for Research in Mathematics*, 1980, *11*, 356–366.

Wylie, R. *The Self-Concept: Theory and Research on Selected Topics*. Vol. 2. Lincoln: University of Nebraska Press, 1979.

Yair, G. "Reforming Motivation: How the Structure of Instruction Affects Students' Learning Experiences." *British Educational Research Journal*, 2000, *26*, 191–210.

JULIAN G. ELLIOTT is professor of educational psychology and associate dean at the School of Education, University of Sunderland, England.

JANINE BEMPECHAT is senior consultant at the Program for Educational Change Agents, Eliot-Pearson Department of Child Development, Tufts University, Medford, Massachusetts.

2

Japanese mothers who were treated harshly as children believed they thereby developed personal strengths and competencies that increased their parenting efficacy once they had their own families.

Parenting Self-Efficacy Among Japanese Mothers: Qualitative and Quantitative Perspectives on Its Association with Childhood Memories of Family Relations

Susan D. Holloway, Kazuko Y. Behrens

Researchers seeking to understand Japanese children's high achievement in school often cite family processes as one key contributor to success (Hess and others, 1986; Holloway, 1988). Some find evidence that Japanese mothers are particularly sensitive and responsive, while others focus on their effectiveness in motivating children to study hard (Rothbaum and others, 2000b; Smith and Wiswell, 1982; Vogel, 1996; Stevenson and Stigler, 1992). Still other analyses of family relations in Japan illuminate weaknesses as well as strengths. For example, compared to mothers in other industrialized countries, Japanese women express little confidence in their parenting abilities (Bornstein and others, 1998; Shwalb, Shwalb, and Shoji, 1996). And recent studies find evidence of problems among Japanese youth, including rising rates of juvenile crime, school truancy, and school violence, as well as evidence of a seven-fold increase in child abuse in the home over the past decade ("Child Abuse Is on the Rise," 2000).

To move beyond these apparent contradictions and paradoxes, research is needed that examines variation in parenting strategies, as well as the conditions that support or undermine Japanese parents in their attempts to socialize and educate their children. Such studies necessarily move away from designs in which the "average native" in Japan is compared with his or her counterpart in another country (Shore, 1996). The study reported in this chapter was designed to take an in-depth look at the varied circumstances of families within Japan. By collecting qualitative and quantitative data before and after the child's transition to first grade, we examined how Japanese mothers from working-class and middle-class backgrounds draw on cultural models of learning and development to support their children's adjustment (see Suzuki, Holloway, Behrens, and Yamamoto, 2001, for an overview of the larger study).

We focus on the factors associated with mothers' sense of efficacy as a parent. Self-efficacy is defined as "beliefs in one's capabilities to organize and execute the courses of actions required to produce given attainments" (Bandura, 1997, p. 3). Although some have questioned the validity of the construct of efficacy in a society where collectivistic norms are said to be dominant, our previous work suggests that Japanese adults are strongly motivated to identify and complete the tasks associated with their role. While an important goal of many Japanese may be to contribute to the welfare of a societal group, this collective orientation does not lessen the individual's motivation to evaluate whether she is capable of accomplishing her individual part effectively (Holloway, 2000). In addition to their own penchant for self-evaluation, Japanese mothers are also held strongly accountable for their children's actions by educators, the media, and politicians (Holloway, 2000). We view the construct of parenting self-efficacy as a culturally transcendent barometer of a woman's own perceptions of her competence in handling the requirements of the culturally constructed role of mother. The elements believed to constitute a good mother vary across societies, as do the structural characteristics that support or undermine parenting self-efficacy, such as economic conditions or social policies governing early childhood education.

In the United States, higher self-efficacy is found among mothers who are well educated, receive adequate social support, and have children who are not difficult (Cutrona and Troutman, 1986; Ozer, 1995; Teti and Gelfand, 1991). In addition, there is some evidence that mothers who have a well-integrated representation of their childhood relationships with their own parents may perceive themselves as more competent (Grusec, Hastings, and Mammone, 1994). Mothers who rate themselves as efficacious parents are less likely to be depressed and more positive in their interactions with their young children; they are also more likely to volunteer in their children's school, participate in school governance, and help their children with homework (Bandura, Barbaranelli, Caprara, and Pastorelli, 1996; Hoover-Dempsey and Sandler, 1997; Silver, Bauman, and Ireys, 1995; Williams and others, 1987).

The study examined here builds on this literature on parenting self-efficacy and extends it to explore conditions and characteristics of contemporary Japanese families. We first report on a series of quantitative analyses designed to examine the association between self-efficacy and mothers' representations of their own childhood relationships with their parents. We then explore data from open-ended interview questions using qualitative methods. These analyses serve to elucidate the ways in which mothers experience their own childhoods, the salient dimensions they use to discuss their own childhoods, and the ways in which their perceptions of their own childhoods are connected to their current parenting.

Quantitative Assessment of Mothers' Representations of Early Experiences

Our quantitative analyses focused on the relationship of parenting self-efficacy to characteristics of the mothers' family of origin. Of particular interest was whether parenting self-efficacy is related to the representations that mothers hold of their own childhood relationships with their parents. According to the attachment paradigm, children develop working models of the self and others that organize their cognitive, social, and affective experiences and have consequences for the quality of subsequent relationships (Bowlby, [1969] 1982). The nature of parents' working models of attachment has been shown to affect their parenting style. Mothers who have not come to terms with early attachment difficulties are likely to be less warm, to provide less structure in interacting with their children, and to feel more helpless and out of control than those who experience others as trustworthy and responsive (Cohn, Cowan, Cowan, and Pearson, 1992; George and Solomon, 1999). Our analysis focuses on the nature of the recalled relationship, including perceptions of parental affection and support; we expected that mothers who perceived their parents as loving and accepting would feel more efficacious in their relationships with their own children.

We were also interested in examining the relationship of self-efficacy to the socioeconomic status of the mother's family of origin. In the United States, wealthier, more educated parents are likely to feel more efficacious, particularly dealing with matters concerning their children's education (Hoover-Dempsey and Sandler, 1997; Lareau, 1989). In Japan, although the range in family income is not as wide as in the United States, there are also class-based differences in parenting beliefs and strategies (Azuma, 1996; Holloway, 2000).

Birth order is another factor related to parenting self-efficacy. In the United States, it appears that firstborns may be given more attention and responsibilities than later-born children, thus developing more internal control beliefs and greater self-efficacy (Schneewind, 1995). In Japan, the effects of birth order may be even stronger because individuals tend to be heavily associated with a role identity, and they are judged according to how well they approximate the ideal type for that role. Within the family, the role of elder sister is particularly well defined; the older girl must act in a mature and responsible manner, care for younger siblings, and eschew the indulgence often accorded to young children (Doi, 1973). We expected that mothers who were firstborns might perceive themselves as more efficacious parents as a result of their early caregiving experiences.

We also examined the issue of gender in the mother's family of origin; we felt that women who had one or more brothers may have felt less valued by their parents and may in turn be less efficacious in their own child rearing compared to women who were raised as only children or with sisters only. It is often claimed that Japanese mothers are more indulgent and tolerant toward sons than toward daughters, a preference that may reflect the traditional role of male heirs in perpetuating the family line (Iwao, 1993; Uno, 1999).

In addition to examining features of the mothers' family of origin, we assessed several characteristics of the contemporary family structure, including the number of children in the family and the gender of the target child. We expected that mothers with more children would feel less efficacious due to their increased workload. We also expected that mothers of boys would feel more efficacious because of the societal emphasis on the special, enjoyable quality of the mother-son relationship.

Participants

We selected forty mothers from Sapporo, a large city in Hokkaido, the northernmost island of Japan. To ensure variation in social class background, we drew half the sample from a low-tuition preschool serving working-class families and half from a relatively expensive one serving middle- and upper-middle-class families. Each preschool director invited the participation of mothers whose children were in the five-year-old class. (In Japan, children attend preschool until age six, when they move into first grade.) The husbands of the respondents whose children attended the low-fee school were employed as semiskilled and skilled manual workers, clerical workers, and small farm or business owners. The majority of husbands of respondents whose children attended the more expensive school were high-level executives and major professionals.

Overall, mothers' education background was fairly evenly divided between those completing high school (40 percent) and those attending junior college or college (45 percent), with a small number who graduated from a vocational program following high school (15 percent). Mothers were primarily from working-class (22.5 percent) or middle-class (55 percent) origins. Just over half (55 percent) had a male sibling. Slightly more than half (58 percent) of the women had more than one child. In almost all cases, the sibling was younger than the target child. In 55 percent of the families, the target child was male. The mothers in this sample were not employed outside the home; in contrast, 43 percent reported that their own mothers had been employed outside the home during the respondents' childhood.

Procedure

Mothers were interviewed individually by a native Japanese speaker in a private room of the preschool. Interviews lasted approximately one hour and were audiotaped. After the interview, participants completed a questionnaire.

The interview contained open-ended questions to assess mothers' (1) representations of their own childhood experiences; (2) views of their preschool-aged child, including current characteristics and expectations for the future; (3) perceptions of their relationship to the child, including affective bond, cognitive stimulation, and preparation for school and discipline; (4) perceived parenting self-efficacy; (5) sources of social support; and (6) plans for the future.

For this chapter, responses regarding mothers' representations of their own childhood experiences were analyzed using both qualitative and quantitative methods. For the quantitative analyses, scores were derived for two scales, Loving Experiences and Rejecting Experiences. The coding scheme was adapted from the adult attachment experience scoring scales (Main and Goldwyn, 1998). The Loving Experiences scale assesses the sense of emotional support and availability of a parent, particularly in times of trouble; indicators include memories of physical love and comfort, of receiving help when upset or frightened, or of doing something bad but being forgiven. The Rejecting Experiences scale assesses the sense of being turned away prematurely or inappropriately; indicators include memories of favoritism to siblings, fears of abandonment, or an absence of affection. Each respondent's interview received a score on a nine-point scale for loving experiences and a second score for rejecting experiences. These scale values do not reflect the extent to which the mother has attempted to understand and come to terms with past events; rather, it is an assessment of the quality of the mother's remembered experiences. Intercoder reliability, computed on ten transcripts, was 80 percent for loving experiences and 90 percent for rejecting experiences.

The self-efficacy questionnaire contained twenty-six parenting items. Questions were included in each of four areas:

1. Promoting cognitive behavior and self-help skills by teaching specific skills (for example, teaching how to count)
2. Promoting social development by teaching conventions (for example, teaching how to greet others appropriately)
3. Fostering a close emotional relationship with the child (for example, understand the child's feelings)
4. Generally monitoring and promoting the child's activities and relationships with others (for example, provide opportunities to play with others)

Mothers were asked to use a six-point scale to rate their self-efficacy on each item. A summary score with high internal reliability was obtained by computing the average rating across all items (coefficient alpha = .86).

Analysis

Descriptive statistics were computed for the total self-efficacy score, experiences scales, and family structure variables. The majority of mothers (70 percent) expressed moderate levels of self-efficacy (scores of 3 or 4), and nearly all the rest (28 percent) gave themselves a 5 or 6, indicative of high self-efficacy. The average score was 4.11 (SD = .57). There was a wide range of experience scores; the average for loving experience was 4.28 (SD = 1.99), and for rejecting experience, the average was 3.00 (SD = 2.17). Nearly 60 percent of mothers had a negative view of their childhood due to either a lack of loving memories or the presence of rejecting memories.

Correlational analyses revealed several relationships among parenting self-efficacy, the socioecological variables, and memories of early relationships. Mothers who were more efficacious were more likely to have only one child and were somewhat more likely to have a boy. Mothers whose fathers' occupations were higher status reported more loving experiences as a child. Mothers who were more highly educated reported having more loving experiences as a child and, marginally, fewer rejecting experiences.

To create a regression model, we entered families of predictors into simultaneous multiple regression analyses. The best model contained three variables and explained 24 percent of the variance. Mothers tended to report higher self-efficacy if they had one child, if their child was a boy, and if they had memories of being more frequently rejected by their own parents.

These findings were surprising in a number of ways. First, in the light of the work by Bornstein and others (1998), we were surprised that many mothers reported feeling relatively efficacious in their parenting. We attribute this in part to the fact that we engaged in a rather lengthy open-ended interview prior to administering the questionnaire. The frank discussions may have put mothers at ease, making them less likely to respond with culturally appropriate modesty, a tendency that has been noted in earlier surveys of Japanese mothers.

We were somewhat surprised that mothers with one child evidenced greater self-efficacy than those who had two or more. However, this finding can be explained by the fact that in almost all of our families, the target child was the elder, so mothers who had two children were dealing with a preschooler and an infant or toddler. It may be that this is a particularly challenging configuration and that mothers' self-efficacy increases as their children grow up and the family passes through this difficult period.

Truly unexpected, however, was how many mothers reported that their childhood experiences had been negative. A further surprise was that the Rejecting Experiences scale was positively (although marginally) correlated with self-efficacy. We had not expected that mothers who reported more rejection would experience greater self-efficacy as parents. Our qualitative analyses were designed to attain a better understanding of this puzzling finding. In particular, we looked in depth at mothers' responses to the following questions:

- How did they experience their own childhoods?
- What are the salient dimensions they use to discuss their own childhoods?

- In what ways are their perceptions of their own childhoods connected to their current parenting?
- How are these experiences related to their evaluations of themselves as parents?

Growing Up in Japan: Mothers' Views

In the open-ended interviews, we began by asking our respondents to describe what their mothers had been like when they—our respondents— were growing up. We probed further by asking whether they ever felt that they had been treated differently from their siblings. We also asked whether there were any ways in which they were doing things differently from their own mother. Our first analysis consisted of an examination of the terms the women used to characterize their mothers.

Perceptions of Their Mothers. One group, constituting nine women, described their own mothers primarily in terms of warmth, kindness, and involvement. These images embody the modal style frequently described in the research literature on Japanese mothers (Rothbaum and others, 2000b). The comments of one mother are typical of this group: "Since I was small, my mother always put the priority on her children. For everything, every time when my parents had some time off, we always went on a trip to some place. I think that kind of mother is a good mother."

For a further eight of the women, their own mothers combined a strict disciplinary style with a fundamental kindness. This balance seemed to be approved of by these mothers or characterized as ordinary. For example, one mother said that her mother "was strict to us three children, but she was also kind. I am still afraid of her sometimes [laugh]. She just never accepted lies. If you lie and she finds out about it, she doesn't speak to you."

The largest group of women (sixteen or forty) characterized their mothers solely as either *kibishii* (strict) or *kowai* (scary). Although a few women perceived this parenting style as positive in its effects, most were critical of their mothers for giving them insufficient attention or affection. We provide an extended list of examples of these descriptions in Exhibit 2.1. The women mention an array of strict and frightening maternal behaviors, including physical punishment, verbal scolding, and demands for good manners and help with household work. Of the remaining seven women in the sample, three described their mothers primarily as being busy, and the others offered idiosyncratic descriptions totally different from the dimensions used by the rest of the group.

Sense of Isolation. A second theme pertained to the women's feeling of isolation from their mothers due to their physical absence or emotional distance. Fourteen women characterized their mothers as busy or hardworking, and nine specifically said that they had been lonely as children.

Exhibit 2.1. Mothers' Descriptions of Their Own Mothers as Being Strict (*Kibishii*) or Scary (*Kowai*)

"When I was a child, I remember feeling that she was scary. I feel that I was always being scolded. Now, today, they say that we should raise our children by praising them. But it wasn't like that. I was scolded or I just wonder if she ever accepted me, when I think back now. It was very strict or tough. My father was very scary. I don't think I ever had a normal conversation with him. In any event, I don't really remember that I was ever loved much at all by my parents, both my mother and my father."

"My mother was very controlling. She was, like, I can't do this, and I can't do that. She was very rigid and really intimidating. Always, even when my friend was bad, I was the one who got scolded, like that. She had a very strong will, and so she could really persevere at things and also didn't know how to ask for indulgence. Maybe she wanted to complain and show her weakness, but she couldn't. So, I thought, like, for things like that, it was her loss. Also for her children, too, she demanded strictness, but like, because I was controlled, maybe I went in the opposite direction."

"She was like a devil. She would scold totally depending on how she felt, and then although she'd get mad based on her feelings, she did insist on what's wrong is wrong, and would stand up with a medal of honor. She was like hysterical. Every day, I kept being scolded in any event. I was spanked, thrown out of the house, beaten with [inaudible], and pushed in water. I mean really! Now if anyone did such a thing, it'll be considered a crime. All my siblings experienced this kind of thing. Now we all laugh at it. Honestly, I didn't like her. I hated and hated her so much."

"She was so strict. Regarding education and child rearing, she wasn't strict, but about playing. . . . She never did anything with children. Well, those days were, it was the period for advanced economic growth. As the name tells, it was the period for work, work, work. Even at harvest time, there was no extra help. She was always yelling. I guess she didn't really have the emotional capacity. And so I resisted and disobeyed. During my rebellious period, I totally hated my parents with all my guts. Everything she said totally ignored my human rights. She said everything, using parental rights as the excuse, 'What do you think you're saying toward your parent?' "

"She was a strict mother, and the economy was really going up. I think there was a period when she wanted to differentiate social class, like 'I'm a little higher class than you are' type of thing. I know there is no class system in Japan, but in those days, I think people were becoming conscious of that kind of thing. So she was looking at or aiming for the upper class, and she told me to behave, to have good manners. So she made me wear traditional clothes, and she was just strict in every aspect."

For example, this woman described numerous hardships created by her mother's heavy workload: "She always worked. Besides her own work as a nurse, she also used to help my father. She was like a superman who flies around in the sky [laughs]. My mother still says today that she doesn't remember educating either of us, me and my brother. I guess that she seems to think that all she was doing was working and housework and couldn't spend much time with her children. She says she never taught us much or engaged in discipline much. She thinks she couldn't care for us much, and she still says that."

Other women had mothers who did not work outside the home but were emotionally distant. For instance, one woman remembered feeling lonely as a result of being neglected by her mother: "She was very active. Also, she was kind of scary. I was scolded often. She seemed to have gone out for pleasure often. When I was a child, I think I did feel lonely sometimes. I was kind of, how can I say it, neglected, brought up neglected." Others described similar experiences of being left alone while their mothers were pursuing their own social or volunteer activities: "Well, frankly, when I was a child, I was totally left alone. She was really a free-spirited woman. She was involved in lots of church activities. So she used to say that I was already old enough to take care of myself and help with household chores. And she sometimes worked as a part-timer. So I was a latchkey child and stayed home alone with my sister since I was very young. With my child, I try to achieve a certain distance and closeness. Well, in my mother's case, it was more like distance and distance [laughs]."

The respondents frequently used the term *gaman,* which means endurance or forbearance, to convey how they endured feelings of loneliness: "She was always busy, so I think we siblings had to really endure a lot. She came home late, so I did feel lonely sometimes." These women felt they had less opportunity to be indulged or pampered (*amayakasu*), a relationship dynamic frequently described as characteristic of Japanese child rearing (Doi, 1973): "My mother had me when she was twenty. So she was a very young mother and I felt like she was my sister or a friend. I couldn't be indulged by her. Objectively, maybe she wasn't really a mother type. But she still was a mother to me."

It is interesting to note the various attributions the respondents made about why their mothers tended to be neglectful or emotionally distant. While many cited economic exigencies (their mothers' need to help support the family), others viewed their behavior as caused by a personality characteristic—a function of their mothers' "free-spirited" nature, their immaturity, or their simply not being a "motherly type." A couple of mothers analyzed the behavior in terms of prevailing cultural models of child rearing during that period in Japan; for example, one woman commented, "Because she was very busy, I don't think my mother was able to look really deeply into her children's feelings. Also, it could be due to the different times. In those days, people used to say, 'Children grow up on their own even if they are left alone.'"

Perceptions of How Siblings Were Treated. In the first couple of interviews, we did not specifically ask the women whether they had been treated differently from their siblings, but they mentioned the issue spontaneously and with such emotion that we began to explore it further in our interviews with the rest of the sample. Of the thirty-seven mothers who had one or more siblings, twenty-five perceived that they had been treated worse than their siblings, seven perceived that they had been treated better, and five thought that the siblings had received similar treatment.

Three reasons were given to explain differential treatment: gender (mentioned by eight mothers), birth order (mentioned by twenty-five mothers), and personality differences (mentioned by eleven mothers). Some mothers cited the general belief that boys were more *kawaii* than girls. *Kawaii* is usually translated as "cute," "endearing," or "darling" if it refers to a person. It refers to a quality that elicits a desire to indulge, pamper, or care tenderly for the person in question. Therefore, it is connected to the notion of *amayakasu* because a child who is *kawaii* seems to elicit indulgence from the parent. Some respondents felt that their parents preferred their cuter brothers and tended to indulge them by giving them more attention and affection, as well as more clothing, toys, vacation opportunities, and the like. As one mother said, "We were both given allowances, you know? I bought clothes because I wanted them. But my brother didn't want any clothes, and he wanted books. Then my mother used to buy clothes for him. Well, I buy clothes, using my allowance, because that is what I wanted. But my brother buys books, and my mother buys him clothes anyway [laughs]. If I think back, you often hear a boy is always a mother's favorite. So maybe she did that because she favored him. Something like that. I felt she was strict only toward me."

Birth order was another powerful reason for differential treatment. Respondents who were the firstborn child felt that they were asked to be mature and independent, while their mothers were sweeter and more indulgent toward younger siblings. They also claimed that they were scolded for any misbehavior, whereas the younger sibling received little blame even when it was warranted. In Exhibit 2.2, we present four examples of mothers who felt they were subjected to differential treatment because they were the older daughter (*oneechan*).

In addition, eleven mothers thought that they elicited different parenting because of their personality, which was itself affected by their position in the family. According to these mothers, the eldest child often becomes, out of necessity, more self-reliant; her parents then use her independence to justify continuing to give more attention to the younger sibling. Some mothers felt that this was an acceptable child-rearing strategy, or they expressed an attitude of resignation toward it, as did this woman: "Well, everybody used to say that I was a strong and mature [*shikkari*] child. So my mother treated me that way. She didn't have to care for me too much because I was doing it right. But my younger brother was spoiled [*amaenbo*] and was very fussy about his likes and dislikes. But I never felt that she paid attention only to my brother. And I felt that it couldn't be helped because he was my little brother."

Some mothers seemed to think that they had been justifiably singled out for worse treatment due to a personal failing: "I do feel my mother treated my sisters differently from me. I did but I thought that it couldn't be helped. I wasn't like my elder sisters. They were really mature. And I wasn't like them, and I probably did things I would be scolded for most often.

Exhibit 2.2. Mothers' Reports of Difficulties Due to Being the Older Daughter (*Oneechan*)

"Oh, my mother would always say, 'because you're *oneechan*.' I sometimes wished my mother would take the situation into account. But even if my brother was the one who did bad things, I was the one who was responsible and who was scolded because I was the older sister."

"My elder brother and I were close in age, and we got along well. But my younger sister was much younger, and she was tomboyish and wild. Because she was the youngest, my mother loved her more than my brother and I. She was given more things [laugh]. So, for something like that, I was envious of her. We were given only one pair of shoes and had to wear them for at least three years. But my sister used to lay out so many pairs of shoes to choose before she went to school and would wonder which ones to pick. But I was a younger sister, too, after all. Because I was the older one, I grew up hearing, 'because you are *oneechan*' and 'because you are *oneechan*' all the time until I got really sick of it. But now that I have two children, too, I think that there is such a term. And so now I do think that because my son is *oniichan* [the eldest brother]. But it's true that he is *oniichan*, you know. So, when I tell him to straighten up, I tell him to straighten up because he is *oniichan*."

"When my sister cried first, I heard my mother saying, 'You're *oneechan*, so. . . .' So, *oneechan* has to endure. Maybe in the old days, I guess that kind of thinking couldn't be helped. So, for my son, I use the 'you're *oniichan*' phrase only when I praise him. That's what I've been trying to do."

I strongly longed to be smart like my sisters. I often wondered why I was the only one who wasn't smart. I wondered why I kept doing stupid things. And, of course, then I thought it was right to be scolded."

Others were not willing to bear the responsibility and believed they had been treated unfairly, including this respondent, who said that her mother had also realized she had expected too much from her oldest daughter: "My mother was weak and often in and out of the hospital. So while she stayed in the hospital, I had to play the mother's role—making dinner, cleaning up, and so forth. So maybe I wasn't very childish or cute; maybe I acted too mature. My mother often did say, 'Being a mother is really tricky. She wants her children to grow up quickly, but also at the same time she wants them to stay as children. So I think I pushed my desire for my children to grow up fast on you and my desire for them to remain as children on your sister.' She has some regrets about that."

In some cases, the respondents believed that their parents were responsible for creating an unhealthy dependence on the part of the indulged child: "We were treated differently by 180 degrees. That was probably because I didn't ask to be pampered as a child. It's often said that parents love the dumber child more, you know. So they are more attentive to the child who can't be independent. I was a child who could do everything by herself, so it's okay. That's what they thought, I think. My mother bought everything for him [my brother], and I guess she loved him very much, but he has no clue, zero sense about money, and he cannot make a living on his own. Then, in the end, my mother is just like a mother bird who feeds her chick, his mouth wide open, 'aaah.'"

This mother highlights the connection between children's position in the family (which is a function of birth order and gender) and their mothers' child-rearing approach. She views the differential early socialization as a factor affecting the children's long-term development. According to this perspective, older sisters are more often expected to work hard and are not indulged as are boys and younger sisters. However, this harsh treatment has the positive effect of helping them become independent and confident in their later relations with their own children.

Implications for Mothers' Child Rearing. It is clear that many mothers resented being treated differently from their siblings because of gender or birth order. When asked what they wanted to do differently from their own mothers, the most common resolution was to avoid treating their children in terms of these positional attributes. Of the thirty-five mothers who stated that they wanted to do something different from their mothers, twelve were determined to avoid favoring a child based on gender or birth order: "When I look at mothers of boys, I see that they will just let them do whatever they want because they are totally cute. So if I were given the opportunity of having a boy in addition to my daughter, I'd try not to favor either child. Both children should be recognized as an individual person rather than trying to blame my daughter, 'You're *oneechan*,' for everything. There may be times that I might say that, you know, when it is true that she's the older sister, and I may ask her to do something for her little brother. But I'll never want to say to her, 'Because you're *oneechan*' for absolutely everything."

In spite of their determination not to differentiate their children according to gender and birth order, some mothers apparently still viewed their children in terms of these roles. For example, one woman expressed the respect developed for her older daughter's willingness to endure the hardships associated with being the elder child:

> Also, she endures a lot. Sometimes I think she doesn't have to do *gaman* that much, but she does. I can almost see tears in her eyes. When I see her like that, I am impressed and think, "What a child!" Being so young . . . She is *oneechan* at home. She is kind to her little sister and thinks that she has to give everything to her. So the little sister is becoming like a dictator. So she [the older child] knows it is unfair, but she endures it. Then she goes to a corner of the room and sobs. But she still doesn't complain. So when I notice something like that, I try to scold the little one and comment, "*Oneechan* is great. She is really enduring everything!"

Some mothers acknowledged the difficulty of reversing this strong emphasis on roles; one frankly acknowledged that she benefited from the efforts of her older son: "At first, we were trying not to call him *oniichan* at home. I was calling him by a nickname and calling the younger one by a nickname too. But around the time he entered preschool, for some reason he started to be called *oniichan*. Then he himself started to act more mature [laughs]. When I couldn't move around too much, I sometimes caught myself asking him to do something for the younger one and realized that I do depend on him."

Capturing the Complexities of Japanese Family Life

The research examined here illustrates an aspect of growing up within a Japanese family that is rarely highlighted in the research literature. Many of the mothers in this sample experienced their parents as demanding and emotionally distant. The expectations placed on them often stemmed from their place in the birth order and their gender. We have seen that the role of eldest daughter, in particular, can be a difficult one, requiring the child to give up a certain amount of affection and attention and take on more responsibilities. Moreover, the elder daughter is expected to do this without complaining and without expressing resentment to the younger siblings. As several mothers mentioned, they felt the injustice of having their own personal characteristics ignored in favor of these positional attributes. They continued to experience anger that they had been deprived of the pleasant experiences apparently provided to their younger siblings.

The anger and resentment that these Japanese mothers felt as children, and continued to feel decades later, remind us that cultural goals are often attained through a process that is contested by some participants within the society. Socialization does not always occur through a process of gentle inducement or harmonious co-construction; rather, the desires of the individual child are sometimes systematically suppressed by parents who desire to create in their child certain culturally desired attributes or who may need the child's cooperation in dealing with the demands of daily life.

Furthermore, these mothers remind us that Japanese children are socialized through a variety of mechanisms. The use of indulgence (*amae*) is one parenting strategy that many researchers have tended to emphasize in describing Japanese parents (Rothbaum and others, 2000a, 2000b). Yet we have seen in this study that withdrawing or withholding indulgence is also common. Firstborn children may grow up receiving little or no indulgence from their parents if a younger sibling is born within a year or two of the elder child. While Japanese mothers may guess at their child's feelings, using the empathy for which they have become known in the research literature (Rothbaum and others, 2000b), they do not always act in ways to alleviate any perceived discomfort. Rather, parents may require emotional suppression on the part of their children to achieve parents' desired social and economic goals. When these expectations are not met, the punishment can be severe.

The Japanese phrase *ame to muchi* (sweetness and the whip) is sometimes used to describe a technique of disciplining children that balances indulgent and demanding practices (Holloway, 2000). It appears that both types of strategy, the sweet and the severe, have been used by Japanese parents for many generations. As historian Kathleen Uno (1991) has noted, traditional parenting strategies during the period from 1600 through the modern period included "patient persuasion, cajoling, moral lecturing, and silent example," as well as "harsher means, such as scolding, physical punishment, confinement in dark storehouses or cages, locking children out of the house, and for extremely intractable children, moxa coauterization (burning dried vegetable powder on the child's skin)" (p. 396). To obtain a clear picture of socialization and education in contemporary Japan, it is important to examine the interplay of indulgence and demandingness over a range of families.

While some mothers in our study appeared resentful of their treatment, others saw it as an inevitable aspect of family functioning. The experience of rejection may have a different meaning for this latter group because differential treatment is viewed as a function of role demands rather than as an expression of personal enmity on the part of their parents. They also saw a positive aspect: they learned about taking care of children and performing household activities. Therein lies the key to the mysterious finding from our quantitative analysis that more efficacious mothers had often experienced more rejection than less efficacious mothers. The Rejecting Experiences score is affected by perceptions of differential treatment by parents among siblings; there were a large number of oldest daughters in the sample, the group most likely to perceive disfavorable treatment and perhaps to be forced to perform tasks that eventually resulted in a feeling of competence as parents—hence, their high scores on the Rejecting Experiences scale and their correspondingly high scores on the parenting Self-Efficacy scale.

We have several hypotheses as to why we found more evidence of harsh treatment and less of indulgence than previous researchers have. The first hypothesis concerns the nature of our sample, which contained many working-class families and was selected from the region of Hokkaido. In contrast, most previous research has examined middle-class parents from the central island of Honshu (Rothbaum and others, 2000b). Hokkaido is a relatively remote rural area that experiences hard winters. Although our sample was recruited from the large city of Sapporo, many of the women had grown up on farms or in small fishing villages throughout Hokkaido. The difficulties of day-to-day life in this demanding environment may foster a stricter and more exigent parenting style, particularly among working-class families. These findings remind us not to ignore the presence of regional and socioeconomic variation in parenting beliefs and child-rearing strategies, even in societies perceived as homogeneous (Gjerde, 1996).

Another hypothesis is that our methodology allowed us to move beyond the more superficial responses that are elicited when respondents are given brief questionnaires. We felt that mothers responded well to the open-ended interview format. They also seemed to feel free to express themselves with an interviewer who shared their national background and language but was living outside Japan. They may have been more willing to reveal socially unacceptable feelings of anger to this culturally knowledge-able quasi-outsider than they would have been to a foreign researcher or a researcher affiliated with a Japanese university.

A third distinctive characteristic of this study was its focus on the respondents' own interpretations of parenting behavior and their emotional reaction to it. In contrast, most work on Japanese parenting has tended to rely on observations (frequently conducted by foreigners) of parenting strategies. These observations cannot completely capture the meaning to the child—or the impact—of a particular strategy. In fact, what appears to be a benign or permissive parenting strategy to an American observer may actu-ally be perceived as quite threatening by the Japanese child. For example, Azuma (1996) has described American misinterpretations of the situation in which a Japanese mother tells her resistant child that he is "free" to con-tinue misbehaving. While Americans might take her statement at face value and view it as a permissive strategy, Azuma argues that she is in fact threat-ening to withdraw her own emotional and instrumental involvement with the child, an action that the child would experience as quite aversive. Of course, the respondents in our study were adults, and they were providing retrospective accounts, which undoubtedly differ from the processing that occurs at the time of the incident. An exciting direction for future research would be to interview children as well; their perspectives are almost entirely missing from the growing literature on Japanese families.

In conclusion, we wish to underline the potential contribution of stud-ies that combine qualitative and quantitative methods, particularly when the research focuses on communities outside the American middle class. In the light of the important insights we obtained from our mixed method design, we hope that educational researchers increase their efforts to include qual-itative approaches in their attempts to understand the connections joining family, school, and community.

References

Azuma, H. "Cross-National Research on Child Development: The Hess-Azuma Collaboration in Retrospect." In D. W. Shwalb and B. J. Shwalb (eds.), *Japanese Childrearing: Two Generations of Scholarship.* New York: Guilford Press, 1996.

Bandura, A. *Self-Efficacy: The Exercise of Control.* New York: Freeman, 1997.

Bandura, A., Barbaranelli, C., Caprara, G. V., and Pastorelli, C. "Multifaceted Impact of Self-Efficacy Beliefs on Academic Functioning." *Child Development,* 1996, *67,* 1206–1222.

Bornstein, M. H., and others. "A Cross-National Study of Self-Evaluations and Attributions in Parenting: Argentina, Belgium, France, Israel, Italy, Japan, and the United States." *Developmental Psychology,* 1998, *34,* 662–676.

Bowlby, J. *Attachment and Loss,* Vol. 1: *Attachment.* New York: Basic Books, 1982. (Originally published 1969.)

"Child Abuse Is on the Rise, Policy, Social Workers Say." *Los Angeles Times,* Mar. 31, 2000, p. 7.

Cohn, D. A., Cowan, P. A., Cowan, C. P., and Pearson, J. "Mothers' and Fathers'

Working Models of Childhood Attachment Relationships, Parenting Styles, and Child Behavior." *Development and Psychopathology,* 1992, *4,* 417–431.

Cutrona, C. E., and Troutman, B. R. "Social Support, Infant Temperament, and Parenting Self-Efficacy: A Mediational Model of Postpartum Depression." *Child Development,* 1986, *57,* 1507–1518.

Doi, T. *The Anatomy of Dependence.* New York: Kodansha International, 1973.

George, C., and Solomon, J. "Attachment and Caregiving: The Caregiving Behavioral System." In J. Cassidy and P. R. Shaver (eds.), *Handbook of Attachment: Theory, Research, and Clinical Applications.* New York: Guilford Press, 1999.

Gjerde, P. F. "Longitudinal Research in a Cultural Context: Reflections, Prospects, Challenges." In D. W. Shwalb and B. J. Shwalb (eds.), *Japanese Childrearing: Two Generations of Scholarship.* New York: Guilford Press, 1996.

Grusec, J. E., Hastings, P., and Mammone, N. "Parenting Cognitions and Relationship Schemas." In J. G. Smetana (ed.), *Beliefs About Parenting: Origins and Developmental Implications.* New Directions for Child Development, no. 66. San Francisco: Jossey-Bass, 1994.

Hess, R. D., and others. "Family Influences on School Readiness and Achievement in Japan and the United States: Overview of a Longitudinal Study." In H. Stevenson, H. Azuma, and K. Hakuta (eds.), *Child Development and Education in Japan.* New York: Freeman, 1986.

Holloway, S. D. "Concepts of Ability and Effort in Japan and the United States." *Review of Educational Research,* 1988, *58,* 327–345.

Holloway, S. D. *Contested Childhood: Diversity and Change in Japanese Preschools.* New York: Routledge, 2000.

Hoover-Dempsey, K. V., and Sandler, H. M. "Why Do Parents Become Involved in Their Children's Education?" *Review of Educational Research,* 1997, *67,* 3–42.

Iwao, S. *The Japanese Woman: Traditional Image and Changing Reality.* Cambridge, Mass.: Harvard University Press, 1993.

Lareau, A. *Home Advantage: Social Class and Parental Intervention in Elementary Education.* Bristol, Pa.: Falmer Press, 1989.

Main, M., and Goldwyn, R. "Adult Attachment Scoring and Classification System." Unpublished manuscript, Psychology Department, University of California, Berkeley, 1998.

Ozer, E. M. "The Impact of Childcare Responsibility and Self-Efficacy on the Psychological Health of Professional Working Mothers." *Psychology of Women Quarterly,* 1995, *19,* 315–335.

Rothbaum, F., and others. "Attachment and Culture: Security in the United States and Japan." *American Psychologist,* 2000a, *55,* 1093–1104.

Rothbaum, F., and others. "The Development of Close Relationships in Japan and the United States: Paths of Symbiotic Harmony and Generative Tension." *Child Development,* 2000b, *71,* 1121–1142.

Schneewind, K. "Impact of Family Processes on Control Beliefs." In A. Bandura (ed.), *Self-Efficacy in Changing Societies.* Cambridge, England: Cambridge University Press, 1995.

Shore, B. *Culture in Mind: Cognition, Culture, and the Problem of Meaning.* New York: Oxford University Press, 1996.

Shwalb, D. W., Shwalb, B. J., and Shoji, J. "Japanese Mothers' Ideas About Infants and Temperament." In S. Harkness and C. M. Super (eds.), *Parents' Cultural Belief Systems: Their Origins, Expressions, and Consequences.* New York: Guilford Press, 1996.

Silver, E. J., Bauman, L. J., and Ireys, H. T. "Relationship of Self-Esteem and Efficacy to Psychological Distress in Mothers of Children with Chronic Physical Illnesses." *Health Psychology,* 1995, *14,* 333–340.

Smith, R. J., and Wiswell, W. L. *The Women of Suye Mura.* Chicago: University of Chicago Press, 1982.

Stevenson, H. W., and Stigler, J. W. *The Learning Gap: Why Our Schools Are Failing and What We Can Learn from Japanese and Chinese Education.* New York: Simon & Schuster, 1992.

Suzuki, S., Holloway, S. D., Behrens, K., and Yamamoto, Y. "Do Japanese Mothers Lack Confidence? Diverse Maternal Beliefs and Efficacy." Paper presented at the biennial meetings of the Society for Research on Child Development, Minneapolis, Minn., Apr. 2001.

Teti, D. M., and Gelfand, D. M. "Behavioral Competence Among Mothers of Infants in the First Year: The Mediational Role of Maternal Self-Efficacy." *Child Development,* 1991, *62,* 918–929.

Uno, K. S. "Japan." In J. M. Hawes and N. R. Hiner (eds.), *Children in Historical and Comparative Perspective: An International Handbook and Research Guide.* Westport, Conn.: Greenwood Press, 1991.

Uno, K. S. *Passages to Modernity: Motherhood, Childhood, and Social Reform in Early Twentieth Century Japan.* Honolulu: University of Hawaii Press, 1999.

Vogel, S. H. "Urban Middle-Class Japanese Life, 1958–1996: A Personal and Evolving Perspective." In D. W. Shwalb and B. J. Shwalb (eds.), *Japanese Childrearing: Two Generations of Scholarship.* New York: Guilford Press, 1996.

Williams, T. M., and others. "Transition to Motherhood: A Longitudinal Study." *Infant Mental Health Journal,* 1987, *8,* 251–265.

SUSAN D. HOLLOWAY is adjunct professor of education at the University of California, Berkeley.

KAZUKO Y. BEHRENS is a doctoral student at the University of California, Berkeley.

3

The beliefs about learning that different cultures have—
that is, cultural models of learning—may influence the
meanings children construct for learning and
achievement.

Learning Models in Different Cultures

Jin Li

Victor came from China to the United States five years ago and is now
attending the seventh grade in a Boston suburban school. When his father
wrote in the "parent comments" box on Victor's report card, which showed
straight A pluses in all subjects, that his son needs to improve himself,
Victor's teacher called and asked, "What more do you want for your son?
He is already the best!" Dumbfounded, his parents mumbled, "But a person
needs to be humble and continue to improve himself in his learning. In
China, parents share the same thing with teachers, and they wouldn't complain like that! Victor is a happy child, and he'd be happier to stay humble."
Is this exchange between these parents and the teacher an isolated event, or
does it reflect essential differences in how people in different cultures think
about learning and achievement? Recent research on culture and learning
shows that the latter is the case.

Research on Cultural Views of Learning

Human learning is a vast topic and has been researched from a great many
perspectives. Recently, cultural differences in beliefs about learning have
received increased attention. Researchers have made important advances in
three relevant areas: views of intelligence, general attitudes toward learning, and motivation for learning and achievement.

   The concept of intelligence, originating from the West, stresses logical-
mathematical and verbal skills (Gardner, 1983; Sternberg, 1985) and is
believed to underlie human learning (Gardner, 1991, Vernon, 1969).
However, views from different cultures have been shown to diverge from
this Western concept. For example, African conceptions emphasize wisdom,

trustworthiness, social attentiveness, and responsibility (Dasen, 1984; Serpell, 1993; Super, 1983; Wober, 1974). Japanese conceptions elaborate on different kinds of social competence, such as sociability and the ability to sympathize with others (Azuma and Kashiwagi, 1987); the Chinese view contains moral notions such as self-cultivation and self-improvement, although both the Japanese and Chinese conceptions share the cognitive dimension with the West (Li, forthcoming a; Yang and Sternberg, 1997). Within the United States, ethnic groups also have different views of intelligence; for example, Latinos regard social competence as part of intelligence more than their Anglo counterparts do, and Cambodians stress hard work and observance of school rules more than the other two groups do (Okagaki and Sternberg, 1993).

General attitudes toward learning across cultures have been examined primarily in the formal setting of school. Research shows that Western students focus more on individual characteristics such as independence, task efficiency, competition (Hess and Azuma, 1991; Varenne and McDermott, 1998), self-esteem, and social competence (Chao, 1996; Harter, 1993; Wentzel and Caldwell, 1997). Japanese students display a strong group orientation, compliance with authority, and thoroughness in their approaches to tasks (DeVos, 1973; Hess and Azuma, 1991; Lewis, 1995). Similarly, Chinese learners have more positive attitudes toward learning and higher standards for achievement than their Western peers do (Stevenson and Lee, 1990; Stevenson and Stigler, 1992). Furthermore, Chinese parents regard high expectation, studying hard, and family sacrifice as highly important for their children's school success (Chao, 1996). Another study (Student Learning Orientation Group, 1987) found that students in Malaysia, Sri Lanka, and India viewed doing well on school exams as an important step in their learning, whereas students in Nigeria regarded both exams and formal learning as of less relevance to their lives.

Achievement motivation was originally defined in the West as a personality trait based on one's sense of independence. Many non-Western cultures, including Latino, Indian, and Chinese, measured by this concept were once claimed to lack achievement motivation (McClelland, 1961, 1963). However, research since has challenged this initial claim. For instance, students in Mexico, a culture characterized as collectivist, were found to possess a high level of achievement motivation. Their Mexican American counterparts, surprisingly, had diminished achievement motivation as they resided longer in the United States, a typical culture that purportedly promotes independence. These students' realization of their disadvantage associated with their ethnicity had more to do with their reduced level of achievement motivation than did their sense of independence (Suárez-Orozco and Suárez-Orozco, 1995).

Other research has presented even more diverse ways in which people from different cultures are motivated to learn and to achieve. For example, Salili, Maehr, and Gillmore (1976) found that while U.S. children showed an outcome bias in judging school performance, their Iranian counterparts stressed the importance of striving itself and good intention regardless of one's level of competence and productivity. Similarly, Western learners have been shown to value ability, whereas their Asian peers favor effort (Hau and Salili, 1991; Stevenson and Stigler, 1992). Even when Western learners attribute their achievement or failure to effort, they view it as an unstable cause (Weiner, 1986). By contrast, Chinese students not only value effort but also regard effort as a stable cause for learning and achievement (Hau and Salili, 1991; Salili and Mak, 1988). More in-depth analysis also has revealed that Japanese learners display culturally specific dispositions such as *seishin*, the mental attitude that helps one to tackle a task (White and LeVine, 1987), and *gambaru*, a "positive orientation toward the intrinsic benefits of . . . persistence" (Holloway, 1988, p. 330; also see Singleton, 1989; White, 1987). Finally, most recent research documents how the unique concepts of *dusha* (soul) and *kulturny* (culture) underlie Russian students' motivation for learning (Hufton and Elliott, 2000).

A Critique of Traditional Research on Learning and Culture

These and many other research findings together make a compelling case that culture is an important source of variation in examining beliefs about learning. Despite these advances and the recognition of culture, we know little about how members of cultures conceptualize learning and achievement. There are at least three reasons for this gap.

First, we still rely heavily on preconceived notions about learning and achievement (a priori and etic), which were derived from Western traditional experimental research and applied straightforwardly to other cultures. Emic views (views of those being studied) of learning have rarely been studied directly (except perhaps the research on Japanese learning and achievement already discussed). For example, the notion of success in learning, originally from the West, is widely used to mean either the realization of one's goal in some larger sense, such as getting a desired job with one's skill mastery, or the completion of a specific task, such as solving a math problem. Regardless of how large the scope is, "success" emphasizes an end or closure of a learning activity that is (most often intentionally) pursued by the person. Although this concept in and of itself is unproblematic, it may cause concerns when it is uncritically applied to cultures where learning may not be viewed as something that has an end to it (for example, the Chinese notion of "one shall learn as long as one lives"). Admittedly, learning in the West is not limited to this kind of segmented process. Still, the concept of success (with "failure" as its imminent but psychologically dreadful opposite) in both research and educational practice means something different from the basic understanding of learning in Chinese culture. The common application of preconceived notions from one culture to another raises concerns because the researcher assumes equal validity as well as equal degree of importance of those concepts in the two cultures. Measuring learning outcomes such as grades cross-culturally and labeling them as success is not to be confused with explaining intentions, purposes, significance, meanings, and processes with the same concept. These latter aspects are likely to be revealed when we consider emic perspectives.

Second, research on learning and achievement has been dominated by culturally specific conceptual frameworks. Research within these frameworks involves dichotomies such as success versus failure, ability versus effort, and intrinsic versus extrinsic motivation on the one hand and discrete, isolated variables (such as intelligence and expectancy) and tasks (such as solving a puzzle) on the other. Although scholars have recognized some problems that arise even examining one culture (Bempechat and Drago-Severson, 1999; Li, 2001a; Varenne and McDermott, 1998), these either-or and discrete views are deeply entrenched in research and education. Human learning and achieving experiences within any culture (including Western cultures) rarely involve only polar ends and isolated processes. These research frameworks reduce the rich but varied ways that humans conceptualize and approach learning. Including cultural differences as part of the inquiry requires even more recognition of the inherent limitations of these frameworks, as well as our effort to go beyond these boundaries. We have much to gain when we embrace and examine complexity.

Third, related to the other two issues is that research also seldom documents what anthropologists term meaning systems or cultural models (D'Andrade, 1995; Harkness and Super, 1996; Quinn and Holland, 1987) of learning (Li, 2001a). Cultural models refer to culturally constructed and shared domains of knowledge that serve to structure and constrain people's experiences, "supplying interpretations" of and "inferences" about those experiences and "goals for action" (Quinn and Holland, 1987, p. 6) in a given culture. Moreover, these anthropologists have also argued and shown that such cultural models exert what D'Andrade (1987, 1992) called "directive force," which motivates and guides people's behavior. Knowledge acquisition is one such cultural meaning system that cannot be fully understood by investigating isolated variables and processes. For example, Chinese culture has been noted to emphasize effort, while the U.S. culture values ability. Aside from the unsettling dichotomous characterization of these two cultures, the general labeling alone gives the impression that these two notions are all there is to know about Chinese and U.S. conceptions of learning and achievement. The larger meaning systems involving people's purposes, values, processes, and social, and even moral, strivings, as well as the relationships among various components, are ignored. To claim that the Chinese favor effort while the Americans emphasize ability is to notice just one part of the complex learning model from each culture. Many dimensions of these cultural learning models remain essentially unexamined.

A New Lens: Cultural Learning Models and Possible Developmental End Points

To address the above issues, I (Li, 2001a, forthcoming *b*) used prototype methods (Shaver, Schwartz, Kirson, and O'Connor, 1987) to tap indigenous conceptions without the preconceived notions. The purpose of the study was to describe what researchers consider developmental end points of cultural learning models as constructed by adults from two very different cultures: the United States and China. Middle-class European American college students (whom I refer to henceforth as U.S. students) and Chinese college students participated in the research.

Method and Data. I began the study by consulting terms referring to learning in both cultures with the highest frequency among its synonyms respectively (the higher the frequency, the more often the term is used by people in that culture) and found that *learn/learning* in English and *xuexi* in Chinese both occupy the highest frequency (Francis and Kucera, 1982; Wang and others, 1986). Then twenty fluent bilinguals translated each term into the other language, with half translating in one direction and the other half the reversed direction. This step led to the discovery that *learn/learning* and *xuexi* were the closest equivalents with a nearly perfect translation. Next, three participants from each culture free-associated words and phrases with the terms, which resulted in generating an initial list of 242 items in English and 145 in Chinese (see Table 3.1 for examples of these items). Twenty more participants were asked to provide additional items to these lists, leading to an expansion of 496 items in English and 478 in Chinese. In order to obtain a core list of these references to learning in each culture (and to exclude idiosyncratic items), sixty participants rated each of these items according to its relevance to learning on a four-point scale, with 1 indicating no relevance and 4 most relevance. This procedure yielded the final list of 203 items in English and 225 in Chinese, which was taken as representing the core conceptions of learning in the two respective cultures. Finally, in order to determine how these conceptions of learning are organized, one hundred participants in each culture sorted, based on similarity in meaning, items from their own culture into groups. Cluster analysis of these sorted groups produced two organizational structures of conceptions of learning (see Li, 2001a, forthcoming *b*, for more details).

Similar Complexity and Organization of Conceptions About Learning. First, both cultures have a similarly large set of conceptions about learning (203 U.S and 225 Chinese). The two models may be what Levy (1973) termed "hypercognized" (highly elaborated) domains in their respective cultures. Both models also contain intricate and nuanced ideas about learning. This is not surprising, considering that both cultures rely heavily on learning, especially in the form of formal schooling, for cultural transmission and renewal.

Table 3.1. Top Twenty Learning-Related Words and Phrases Nominated and Rated by U.S. and Chinese Adults

Rank Order	U.S. Items	Chinese Items
1	Study	Keep on learning as long as one lives (lifelong learning)
2	Thinking	Read extensively
3	Teaching	Learn assiduously
4	School	Read books
5	Education	Diligent (in one's learning)
6	Reading	Extensive knowledge and multifaceted ability
7	Teacher	Study
8	Books	Make a firm resolution to study
9	Critical thinking	Study as if thirsting or hungering
10	Brain	There is no boundary to learning
11	Discovery	Concentrate on learning
12	Understand	Eager to learn
13	Information	Take great pains to study
14	Knowledge	Seek knowledge
15	Motivation	The learned understands reasoning
16	Library	Study abroad
17	Students	Do one's utmost to self-study
18	Learn by doing	Learning without thinking is labor lost; thinking without learning is perilous (Confucius)
19	Applying ideas	After learning, one understands that one's knowledge is inadequate (Confucius)
20	Communication	Long-term diligence is the road to the mount of knowledge; endurance of hardship is the boat to the boundless sea of learning

Second, the two conceptual maps show a very similar mental structure, indicating that people in these two cultures classify ideas about learning into similar levels: higher, more abstract categories on top called "superordinate level," less abstract categories in the middle called "basic level," and more specific categories at the bottom called "subordinate level." This kind of mental structure (classification of categorical domains such as natural objects or emotion knowledge) has been demonstrated to be basic to human mental functioning and therefore is believed to be similar across cultures (Rosch, 1975). These data and analysis lend additional support for this theory.

Different Meanings. Meanings of the categories and relationships are vastly different, in fact so different that there is little overlap. This is surprising considering that people in both cultures go to school for a similar length of time and learn similar school curriculum (math, science, and language, with Chinese children beginning to learn English in third grade). A perusal of the top twenty items on both lists in Table 3.1 is informative about the nature of the differences. Linguistically, the U.S. list contains mostly single and regular words (for example, *study* and *books*), whereas most Chinese items (92 percent) have multiple words with many modifiers and idiomatic expressions, including proverbs and sayings (for example, "keep on learning as long as one lives") compared to only 26 percent on the U.S. list. With respect to conceptual features, the U.S. list displays quite a few references to external factors such as resources, institutions, and teaching activities, but the Chinese list has few such references (18 percent versus 3 percent). Moreover, the U.S. list possesses many ideas about thinking, mental processes, and inquiry; the Chinese shows few such concepts (28 percent versus 9 percent). Most striking of all is the near absence of references to hard work, effort, and persistence on the U.S. list. By contrast, such concepts are abundant on the Chinese list (30 percent versus 2 percent). Another noteworthy feature is the strong affect indicating desire and passion on the Chinese list (for example, "Make a firm resolution to study"), while there is a relative lack of affect on the U.S. list. Finally, the Chinese concepts convey a clear call for action (for example, "Do one's utmost to self-study"), thus exhibiting perhaps a stronger tendency of the so-called directive force (D'Andrade, 1987, 1992), but this tendency is less pronounced (perhaps implicit) on the U.S. list.

With respect to actual sorted meanings, the U.S. organizational structure begins with two large groups (superordinate level) labeled "learning processes" and "learning content." The first group contains almost five times as many items as the second group. The size of the groups here could be interpreted as signaling a higher degree of both importance and complexity regarding the various dimensions of learning in the United States. The several intermediate groups (basic level) underneath each of the two groups are divided into another two types: learner characteristics and social context. The learner characteristics group consists of four dimensions: (1) specific processes (such as mental activities), (2) the learner's inner qualities (such as intelligence and motivation), (3) resources (such as books), and (4) developmental foundations. At the same basic level, social context consists of two dimensions: (1) types of school and (2) people in teaching. The map's second largest group, learning content (parallel to learning processes), contains various subjects that learners acquire, such as math and history.

Unlike the U.S. content, the Chinese organizational structure begins with the largest sorted meanings of "desirable approach" and "undesirable approach," where values and preferences are clearly expressed regarding what approach to learning is desirable and what is not (compared to the relatively neutral nature of the U.S. dimensions). Similar to its U.S. counterpart, the Chinese desirable approach contains six times more items than the undesirable approach. The two basic-level groups under the desirable approach are "seeking knowledge" and "achievement." "Seeking knowledge" contains four dimensions: (1) "heart and mind for wanting to learn" (an indigenous Chinese term used to describe one's desire for learning), (2) learning methods (such as strategies and steps), (3) purposes of learning (such as contribution to society), and (4) relationships between teachers and students. Again like the U.S. map, "achievement" at the same basic level also has two significant dimensions: (1) paths and tools (such as examination and bookstore) and (2) different kinds of achievement (such as breadth and depth of knowledge and moral integrity). The superordinate group "undesirable approach" indicates warnings, negatives, and taboos to be avoided in learning (for example, shallowness and lack of desire).

Juxtaposing the two cultures' learning categories, it is apparent that U.S. and Chinese conceptions about learning are quite different despite the similarity in complexity and organization of the respective conceptions.

Under most of these basic-level groups of each culture's model are distinguishable subordinate components where the actual words and phrases are located. A more detailed discussion is needed to bring to the light specific differences regarding the categories noted. Although each model contains many more noteworthy details, this chapter highlights the most significant components for each model (see Li, forthcoming *b*, for a full discussion). The significance level in this analysis was determined by the size of the groups. Thus, the U.S. subordinate components from three of the groups—"specific learning processes," "individual characteristics," and "learning content"—stand out because these have most items in them (35 percent, 17 percent, and 17 percent of the 203 total items, respectively). Three Chinese subordinate components also stand out: "heart and mind for wanting to learn," "purposes of learning," and "kinds of achievement" (28 percent, 12 percent, and 20 percent of the 225 total items, respectively).

Most Significant U.S. Conceptions About Learning. The U.S. "specific learning processes" group, the largest of all groups, contains four distinct but also related components. Items in the first component, active learning, center around the notion that learning is a process in which a person needs to be actively involved, as indicated in the phrases "hands-on" and "learn by doing." The second component, thinking, concerns the mental processes that play an essential role in performing remarkable but finely differentiated feats—for example, "contemplating" and "deductive/inductive" reasoning. The third component, inquiry, stresses how one tries to find out about things in the world through a variety of mental and other activities (for example, "relating ideas"), as well as how one exercises critical thinking in these activities (for example, "challenging assumptions"). Finally, the fourth component, communicating, emphasizes the communicative aspect as an integral part of the learning process that is participatory and interactive but also with a critical attitude toward the process conveyed in terms such as *debate* and *critique*. These and many other ideas in this basic group are core notions of the Western discourse on learning and education (Bruner, 1996; Gardner, 1999; Perkins, 1995). Although each of these four components focuses on a certain set of notions, they are also interrelated. All seem to denote the very active nature of mental processes and inquiry-oriented activities that underlie Western conceptions of learning.

The second most significant group, "individual characteristics," contains conceptions that indicate internal qualities that individual learners possess and are regarded as an essential part of the human capacity for learning. Four distinguishable components emerged. The first, cognitive skill, shows concepts such as memory and focus that learners can use or manipulate for any learning tasks. The second component, motivation, refers to motivational aspects, for instance, ambition and commitment. These notions are essential to achievement motivation, which usually has been studied as individual characteristics of the person, particularly with respect to his or her goals (Maehr and Pintrich, 1991, 1997). The third component, open-mind/creativity, shows ideas about creativity in learning, such as open-mindedness and imagination. This dimension of the learner is widely recognized in research and education, as well as by laypeople. In fact, the West, especially the United States, carries a reputation for fostering open-mindedness, imagination, and creativity (Gardner, 1989). The final component, intelligence, displays different forms of intelligence, such as "booksmart," "wisdom," and "street-smarts." Of the four personal characteristics, these finely differentiated notions of intelligence are central to Western learning (Ogbu, 1994; Varenne and McDermott, 1998).

The third largest U.S. group, subjects of learning, contains a long list of school subjects, types of knowledge, and fields of inquiry. These break into two sets, with the first being basic skills, such as reading and basic arithmetic, and the second being more strictly "school subjects" such as algebra, biology, and literature. All of these bodies of knowledge are the content that the entire group of learning processes aims at acquiring.

Most Significant Chinese Conceptions About Learning. The largest Chinese group is "heart and mind for wanting to learn." As this native term suggests, this group addresses conceptions of personal causality. Four distinct but interrelated components emerged. The first, lifelong pursuit, expresses ideas about one's need to pursue lifelong learning (for example, "there is no boundary to learning" and "upon great achievement, make still further progress"). The second component reveals a four-part disposition: diligence, hardship, steadfastness, and concentration. Diligence refers to the frequency of studying behavior, emphasizing much time spent on learning, as exemplified by "always have a book in one's hand." Endurance of hardship focuses on overcoming difficulties, especially physical drudgery and poverty (for example, "Zhu Maicheng studied while woodcutting—too poor to go to school"). Learning in Chinese tradition is rarely thought of as fun (but "fun" is on the U.S. list) or entertainment, as may be the case with European Americans (Chao, 1996). Instead, it is viewed as a seriously disciplined activity that presents challenges and difficulties, even an "ordeal" for developing character (Lee, 1996; Li, 2001a; Mencius, 1970), as attested to by phrases such as "endurance of hardship is the boat to the boundless sea of learning." Steadfast perseverance is believed to be important because knowledge does not come about overnight, but through a bit-by-bit, accumulative process over a long period of time (Lee, 1996). Steadfastness is required to achieve any serious learning, as exemplified in the phrases, "It takes more than one cold day for the river to freeze three feet deep" and "Without accumulating small steps, one cannot reach a thousand miles." Finally, concentration is used to describe a general learning behavior (across specific tasks) that emphasizes studying with consistent resolution and dedication (for example, "put one's heart into one's study"). Concentration is held as an essential ingredient of Chinese "heart and mind for wanting to learn" because it can ensure a fully engaged mind and heart in the study (Yang, 1979).

The third component in this basic group is humility, which is regarded as a basic orientation toward learning in the Confucian model (Kwok and Lytton, 1996; Lee, 1996; Li, 2001a; Tu, 1979; Wu and Lai, 1992). It refers to a mind-set that regards people as always in need of improving themselves, always ready to be taught and to seek learning (for example, "modest people learn much as little; complacent people learn little as much"). The last component, desire, refers to an enduring and inner desire for learning (for example, "heart and mind for wanting to learn").

The second most significant Chinese group, purposes of learning, has three components that address people's reasoning concerning why they seek knowledge and what benefits they gain from learning. The first one, learning as an end in itself, refers to the notion that learning is essential to being human (for example, "a knife will rust without sharpening," "a person will fall backwards without learning"). The second subgroup, status, conveys that learning can benefit the person for practical purposes—either gaining social status and material benefits or bringing honor to one's family (for example, "learn well and then become an official" and "with math, physics, and chemistry well learned, one has no fear going anywhere"). The third component, contribution to society, reveals the idea that social consciousness and serving the community are part and parcel of one's learning (for example, "cultivate personal life, regulate familial relations, order the affairs of the state, and bring peace and stability to all of the world").

The ideas contained in this basic group are central to Confucian teaching. Accordingly, pursuit of learning is held as the only path toward the highest goal of Confucianism: self-perfection. Obtaining status and bringing honor to oneself and one's family are not contradictory to searching for a higher meaning of life because one's own learning is not only an individual but also a profoundly social process. Therefore, contributing to society is seen as necessary for completing the cycle of self-perfection (Lee, 1996; Li, 2001a; Tu, 1979; Wu and Lai, 1992).

The third most significant Chinese group, kinds of achievement, shows concepts that refer to the consequences of seeking knowledge. There are also four subordinate components. The first, breadth and depth, emphasizes the extensiveness as well as deep understanding of a subject and genuine scholarship (for example, "extensive knowledge and profound scholarship"). The second, extraordinary abilities (for example, "able to recite something after reading it over once"), indicates that the Chinese consider ability to be a subgroup of achievement instead of a cause of achievement or an inherent trait (as it is commonly viewed in the West). Knowing and morality, the third subordinate component, emphasizes the unity between learning and one's moral character (for example, "a student of good character and scholarship"). The fourth, originality, refers to one's creativity (for example, "original view").

Interpretations of the Two Learning Models. Few shared meanings exist between these two cultural models, with each focusing on entirely different aspects of learning (this is also true across the remaining categories that are not discussed in this chapter). Admittedly, there may be some isolated similarities—for example, between the U.S. "motivation," "commitment," "memory," and "creativity" and the Chinese "heart and mind for wanting to learn," "make a firm resolution to study," "able to recite something after reading it over once," and "original view," respectively. Still, large differences exist mainly because these U.S. items emerged as learner characteristics closely related to one's cognitive skills and personality traits. The Chinese items belong to the group singly and signify attitudes, desires, related behaviors, and achievement.

Taken together, the U.S. learning model (representing Caucasian middle- and upper-middle-class members) basically presents a view of learning as a process by which individuals' minds acquire what is out there. Knowledge exists as a more or less neutral body (as embodied by the large number of school subjects) that the minds of individuals can acquire. The conceptual focus is on the distinction between this neutrally existing knowledge body and the internal characteristics of the individual that enable the person to acquire it. The internal learner characteristics include cognitive skill, intelligence, and abilities, on the one hand, and thinking, communicating, and active engagement in the learning processes, on the other. Motivational factors such as interest, curiosity, willingness, and commitment are also part of the internal makeup of a person that serves to facilitate the learning process. The social context is the setting, typically the formal one of school.

This view of learning and knowledge is consistent with the well-established tradition of Western epistemology where knowledge addresses basic questions: What is out there to be known by the mind? What knowledge is reliable? How does the mind know it? How can it be best taught from the perspective of education (Bruner, 1987; Piaget, 1952; Russell, 1945; Scheffler, 1965)? To be sure, some scholars have recently raised issues about whether beliefs about learning ought to be considered as part of epistemology (Hofer and Pintrich, 2001). This view may be important in differentiating motivational aspects from more cognitively oriented construals of knowledge. However, the findings of the study examined here point to the neutral construal of knowledge and learning. Clearly, although learning is an important part of the lives of the Western subjects studied, it does not seem to evoke passionate affect or to be intimately connected to the emotional, spiritual, or moral lives of the respondents. Thus, it is reasonable to suggest that the U.S. view of learning may show a "mind orientation" toward learning.

Members of the Chinese culture may view learning as a personal relationship that the individual builds to knowledge. Unlike the Western construal, the Chinese regard knowledge as something that is indispensable to their personal lives—something that creates meaning for their lives, without which human lives would be unthinkable. This view is also consistent with the age-old understanding of knowledge based on Confucian thought. Knowledge includes not only the externally existing body but also social and moral knowing. The scientific agenda of knowing the world is not the ultimate purpose. Although the Chinese, like the Americans and members of other cultures (Ogbu, 1994; Serpell, 1993; Suárez-Orozco and Suárez-Orozco, 1995), also endorse utilitarian benefits as part of their motivation for learning, their purpose does not end there. Individuals also seek learning in order to cultivate themselves as a whole toward self-perfection beyond the specifics of knowledge and utilitarian ends (Li, 2001a, 2002; Yu, 1996). Chinese beliefs about learning therefore seem to display a person orientation, which elaborates on personal causation of learning (Li, Yue, and Yuan, 2001). As a result, knowledge is not something that Chinese lives can do without; it is something that they must have. This need of knowledge and the seeking of it require that Chinese cultivate the desire to learn, engage in lifelong learning, remain humble, and adopt an action plan of diligence, endurance of hardship, steadfast perseverance, and concentration. Unlike the Western mind orientation, the Chinese person orientation addresses the fundamental questions of what knowledge means to one as a sociocultural being, why one needs to learn it, what one needs to do to learn it and learn it well, and what would happen if one does not learn it. This kind of learning aims at breadth and depth of knowledge, the unity of knowing and morality, practical benefits for oneself and one's family, and contributions to society (Lee, 1996; Li, 2001a, forthcoming a; Tu, 1979; Wu and Lai, 1992; Yu, 1996).

The findings produced by this study may help illuminate the clash between Victor's parents and his teacher. Victor's parents operated quite consistently within the Chinese learning model, where a child's report card is only a signpost on his road to lifelong learning. Because his life is about ongoing striving toward self-perfection, it is, reasoned his parents, important for Victor to remain humble and continue to self-improve. When it comes to learning, there is in their minds no such a thing as "you are the best in class, and therefore you may relax." However, the teacher, based on his comments, may have not understood this Chinese learning model and took the attitude of Victor's parents as psychologically problematic. Probably this incident is not an isolated event but reflects deeper meanings people in different cultures construct about learning.

Developmental Indications

The differences explored here could be viewed as developed forms of learning models in these two cultures. Given these so-called developmental end points, a further question arose as to how children develop these models of learning in their respective cultures. To pursue this research question, my research team (Li, 2001b) began examining U.S. and Chinese preschoolers' understanding of learning (this research is ongoing). Our purpose was to discern emergent thoughts and feelings about learning in these two cultures.

We collected data from 240 children aged three though six, half from China and half from European American backgrounds and half boys and half girls (all from the middle and upper middle class with at least one parent who was college educated). We first showed the children a series of pictures accompanied by a narration depicting a cow that, on seeing a book, decides either to play with a ball or to read the book. Children were asked to pick their preferred ending of the story. They were also shown familiar learning scenarios (a child who is either eager or not eager to go to school and a bird that tries hard to learn how to fly or a bear that gives up on catching fish) with the accompaniment of story beginnings and were asked to complete them.

Preliminary analysis of the five year olds' responses to the cow story indicates that more than twice as many Chinese (60 percent versus 23 percent) chose the book as opposed to the ball option. Moreover, among those who chose the book, more than twice as many Chinese children gave learning and knowledge–related reasons (60 percent versus 27 percent).

In addition, we identified five types of benefits that the children's responses revealed about reading books:

Intellectual benefits. The children's responses referred to learning, increasing one's knowledge, skill, making one smart, and the like—for example, "so you will learn things" (a U.S. response) and "so I can grow knowledge" (a Chinese response).

Language use. The responses contained children's ideas about words, reading, and writing and what they do with them—for example, "you learn how to read."

Achievement-based status and respect. The ideas stated highly desirable statuses and respect people gain with learning and education—for example, "you can become a Ph.D." or "a scientist," and "I want to surpass my teacher" (both Chinese).

Social sharing of knowledge. The responses referred to learning and helping others with the child's skill—for example, "you'd not grow big if you can't help others when they ask you about something" and "when kids are fighting, we can tell them why it's not good to fight" (both Chinese).

Material benefits. The responses concerned ideas that aim at making money, buying desirable things, or getting a good job.

Again, Chinese children expressed significantly more intellectual benefits than did their U.S. peers (94 percent versus 17 percent), and many Chinese, but few U.S. children mentioned the remaining types of benefits. However, many U.S. (but few Chinese) children referred to language use, where they showed remarkable understanding of learning words, how to read and write, and creative ways to use their literacy skills (for instance, "I can get ideas from books and draw people").

With regard to children's responses to the two stories about a child who is eager or not eager to go to school, large differences also emerged. Although both U.S. and Chinese children liked the protagonist who wanted to go to school, many more Chinese (96 percent versus 25 percent) did so for learning-related reasons (for example, "because she loves to learn"). Most U.S. (70 percent) but no Chinese children liked the protagonist for nonlearning and nonsocial reasons (for example, "I like his haircut"). The majority of U.S. children (70 percent) still liked the protagonist who did not want to go to school but gave non-learning-related reasons (for example, "she is pretty"). By contrast, most Chinese children (75 percent) did not like the protagonist for his or her lack of desire to learn compared to only 2 percent of U.S. children who did so.

As a common finding, children from both cultures expressed positive affect toward school and had sophisticated ideas and feelings about school. Consistent with the cow story, however, Chinese children showed a higher frequency of every kind of benefit from learning, knowledge about school, and awareness of social support for their learning (for example, "Mommy says, 'My son, you need to go to school to learn. If you don't, you will not know a lot when you grow up. Mommy will be sad'") than their U.S. peers. Furthermore, Chinese but no U.S. children made references to achievement-based status/respect (for example, "so you can become a Ph.D."). Interestingly, many U.S. but very few Chinese children identified "making friends/playing with them" as a main reason for going to school.

Overall, these preliminary findings seem to show resemblance of the two cultures' learning models, although Chinese children showed more resemblance than U.S. children. Chinese children expressed highly positive and consistent values about learning. Whether these children liked the protagonist was associated directly with whether the protagonist desired learning. This tendency is not only consistent with their adult model, which contrasts their "desirable" against their "undesirable" approach to learning, but it also reveals the degree of importance learning assumes in these children's lives (to the degree that their social relations—liking or not liking their peers—are influenced by their learning model). In addition, Chinese children identified more types of benefits for themselves as well as benefits for others from learning (for example, "if kids are fighting, we can tell them why they should not fight" or "if people don't understand something and ask you, you can tell them, so they'll know"). They also revealed more knowledge about learning in school, such as listening to the teacher, paying attention, and making effort. Finally, they showed more awareness of social support for their learning by frequently imitating their parents' voices of expectations and persuasion (for example, "Mommy says, 'If you don't learn, you won't know a lot'" or "Mommy says, 'You must go to school, or you'll beg on the street'"). These trends again seem coherent with the emphasis of the Chinese model on linking learning to one's whole life development (person orientation) including not just the intellectual but also the socioeconomic, social, moral, attitudinal, and behavioral course of learning.

There also seem to be some emergent themes from the U.S. model. First, for U.S. children, desire or lack of desire for learning is not a reason for liking or not liking someone. Most children liked the protagonist regardless of positive or negative valence of this particular domain of life. We could interpret this tendency as suggestive of children's socioemotional life being somewhat detached from learning (that is, school), which is coherent with the relative emotional neutrality observed in the U.S. adult learning model. These children also identified fewer benefits from learning (to the exclusion of several Chinese categories, such as achievement-based status/respect for learning, material benefits, and, to a large extent, social benefits for others). Again, this could be taken as indicative of learning being viewed as a less encompassing activity and process for their lives. Although for many U.S. children, the utilitarian purposes of schooling will soon be a familiar theme throughout their school career, this dimension is absent in both the adult model and younger children's understanding of learning. Perhaps Americans have more differential views of the process of learning and schooling than the Chinese, therefore attaching different meanings to these processes.

U.S. children made six times more references to making and playing with friends as a main reason that they go to school. Although this theme was not a dimension in the U.S. adult model, fun was. Embedded in the children's references was also the notion of fun, which has been noted as a strong goal for school success among European American but not Chinese mothers of preschool children (Chao, 1996).

The most salient feature of the U.S. model—the heavy emphasis on the mental functioning (mind orientation)—was not explicitly and systematically reflected in the children's references despite isolated acknowledgment that learning can make one smart. Perhaps this part of the understanding of learning is yet to develop among U.S. children. Nevertheless, U.S. children elaborated on one additional dimension that their Chinese peers rarely, if at all, mentioned: language learning and its creative use (for example, "I can write a book" or "you can get ideas from books and act them out"). The attention to imagination and creativity in this area reflects the same emphasis in their adult model. Here, children's understanding does show their awareness of the mental and the mind's prowess to manipulate the symbolic world of the print.

Conclusion

This chapter presents cultural learning models as constructed and expressed by people themselves in their own cultures (emic) as a useful perspective on human learning. Although all humans are endowed with capacities to learn and most of them go to school, their understanding of learning may still differ substantially due to cultural values and priorities.

These cultural learning models are meaning systems that are not reducible to single notions of intelligence, discrete or dichotomous concepts such as ability versus effort and success versus failure, or traditional delineations of achievement motivation. Both the U.S. and Chinese models reveal many more conceptions about learning than these common characterizations of each culture's learning mode. Clearly, the U.S. elaboration of the mental functioning, active nature of engagement, social context, and learning content cannot be reduced to the notion of ability. In the same way, the complex relations about personal conviction, purpose, agency, and achievement conceptions of the Chinese cannot be condensed to the single notion of effort either. Cultural learning models are larger systems of influence, and their complexity merits careful examination.

Researchers studying culture and psychology generally agree that there is no one-to-one correspondence between a given cultural model and individuals' own models and that individuals appropriate, negotiate, and even reject cultural models (Spiro, 1987; Strauss, 1992). Nonetheless, as LeVine (1999) recently argued, cultural impact is evident and acknowledged even when individuals oppose it. So long as children are socialized in their own cultural contexts, their cultures' learning models are bound to exert a so-called directive force to their thinking, feelings, behavior, and outcome of learning (D'Andrade, 1992).

Inquiry into cultural learning models needs to continue. Previous research has provided some important glimpses at parts of these models in various cultures, but they generally fall short of addressing them systematically. The empirical research presented in this chapter seeks to describe these meaning systems from two distinct cultures and to document their early beginnings as young children develop them. The findings confirm the conceptual position that learning models are complex meaning systems, that they differ from culture to culture, and that children begin developing them early in life. Understanding these models and their development may be essential in explaining children's motivation for and ultimate achievement of learning in diverse cultures.

References

Azuma, H., and Kashiwagi, K. "Descriptors for an Intelligence Person: A Japanese Study." *Japanese Psychological Research*, 1987, *29*, 17–26.

Bempechat, J., and Drago-Severson, E. "Cross-National Differences in Academic Achievement: Beyond Etic Conceptions of Children's Understandings." *Review of Educational Research*, 1999, *69*, 287–314.

Bruner, J. *Actual Minds, Possible Worlds.* Cambridge, Mass.: Harvard University Press, 1987.

Bruner, J. *The Culture of Education.* Cambridge, Mass.: Harvard University Press, 1996.

Chao, R. K. "Chinese and European American Mothers' Views About the Role of Parenting in Children's School Success." *Journal of Cross-Cultural Psychology,* 1996, *27,* 403–423.

D'Andrade, R. "A Folk Model of the Mind." In D. Holland and N. Quinn (eds.), *Cultural Models in Language and Thought.* Cambridge, England: Cambridge University Press, 1987.

D'Andrade, R. G. "Schemas and Motivation." In R. G. D'Andrade and C. Strauss (eds.), *Human Motives and Cultural Models.* Cambridge, England: Cambridge University Press, 1992.

D'Andrade, R. *The Development of Cognitive Anthropology.* Cambridge, England: Cambridge University Press, 1995.

Dasen, P. R. "The Cross-Cultural Study of Intelligence: Piaget and the Baoulé." *International Journal of Psychology,* 1984, *19,* 407–434.

DeVos, G. A. *Socialization for Achievement: Essays on the Cultural Psychology of the Japanese.* Berkeley: University of California Press, 1973.

Francis, N. W., and Kucera, H. *Frequency Analysis of English Usage: Lexicon and Grammar.* Boston: Houghton Mifflin, 1982.

Gardner, H. *Frames of Mind.* New York: Basic Books, 1983.

Gardner, H. *To Open Minds.* New York: Basic Books, 1989.

Gardner, H. *The Unschooled Mind.* New York: Basic Books, 1991.

Gardner, H. *The Disciplined Mind.* New York: Simon & Schuster, 1999.

Harkness, S., and Super, C. M. (eds.). *Parents' Cultural Belief Systems: Their Origins, Expressions, and Consequences.* New York: Guilford Press, 1996.

Harter, S. "Causes and Consequences of Low Self-Esteem in Children and Adolescents." In R. F. Baumeister (ed.), *Self-Esteem: The Puzzle of Low Self-Regard.* New York: Plenum, 1993.

Hau, K. T., and Salili, F. "Structure and Semantic Differential Placement of Specific Cases: Academic Causal Attributions by Chinese Students in Hong Kong." *International Journal of Psychology,* 1991, *26,* 175–193.

Hess, R. D., and Azuma, M. "Cultural Support for Schooling: Contrasts Between Japan and the United States." *Educational Researcher,* 1991, *20,* 2–8.

Hofer, B. K., and Pintrich, P. R. *Personal Epistemology: The Psychology of Beliefs About Knowledge and Knowing.* Mahwah, N.J.: Erlbaum, 2001.

Holloway, S. D. "Concepts of Ability and Effort in Japan and the United States." *Review of Educational Research,* 1988, *58,* 327–345.

Hufton, N., and Elliott, J. "Motivation to Learn: The Pedagogical Nexus in the Russian School: Some Implications for Transnational Research and Policy Borrowing." *Educational Studies,* 2000, *26,* 115–122.

Kwok, D. C., and Lytton, H. "Perceptions of Mathematics Ability Versus Actual Mathematics Performance: Canadian and Hong Kong Chinese Children." *British Journal of Educational Psychology,* 1996, *66,* 209–222.

Lee, W. O. "The Cultural Context for Chinese Learners: Conceptions of Learning in the Confucian Tradition." In D. A. Watkins and J. B. Biggs (eds.), *The Chinese Learner.* Hong Kong: Comparative Education Research Centre, 1996.

LeVine, R. "An Agenda for Psychological Anthropology." *Ethos,* 1999, *27,* 15–24.

Levy, R. I. *Tahitians.* Chicago: University of Chicago Press, 1973.

Lewis, C. C. *Educating Hearts and Minds: Reflections on Japanese Preschool and Elementary Education.* Cambridge, England: Cambridge University Press, 1995.

Li, J. "Chinese Conceptualization of Learning." *Ethos,* 2001a, *29,* 1–28.

Li, J. "Understanding of Learning Among U.S. and Chinese Preschoolers." Paper presented at the biennial meetings of the Society for Research in Child Development, Minneapolis, Minn., Apr. 19, 2001b.

Li, J. "A Cultural Model of Learning: Chinese 'Heart and Mind for Wanting to Learn.'" *Journal of Cross-Cultural Psychology,* 2002, *33*(3), 246–267.

Li, J. "High Abilities and Excellence: A Cultural Perspective." In L. V. Shavinina and M. Ferrari (eds.), *Beyond Knowledge: Extracognitive Facets in Developing High Ability.* Mahwah, N.J.: Erlbaum, forthcoming *a*.

Li, J. "U.S. and Chinese Cultural Beliefs About Learning." *Journal of Educational Psychology*, forthcoming *b*.

Li, J., Yue, X.-D., and Yuan, S. "Individual Self and Social Self in Learning Among Chinese Adolescents." Paper presented at the biennial meetings of the Society for Research in Child Development, Minneapolis, Minn., Apr. 21, 2001.

Maehr, M. L., and Pintrich, P. R. (eds.). *Advances in Motivation and Achievement.* Vol. 7. Greenwich, Conn.: JAI Press, 1991.

Maehr, M. L., and Pintrich, P. R. (eds.). *Advances in Motivation and Achievement.* Vol. 10. Greenwich, Conn.: JAI Press, 1997.

McClelland, D. C. *The Achieving Society.* New York: Van Nostrand Reinhold, 1961.

McClelland, D. C. "Motivational Pattern in Southeast Asia with Special Reference to the Chinese Case." *Journal of Social Issues*, 1963, *19*, 6–19.

Mencius. *Mencius.* (D. C. Lao, trans.). Harmondsworth, England: Penguin Books, 1970.

Ogbu, J. U. "From Cultural Differences to Differences in Cultural Frame of Reference." In P. M. Greenfield and R. Cocking (eds.), *Cross-Cultural Roots of Minority Child Development.* Mahwah, N.J.: Erlbaum, 1994.

Okagaki, L., and Sternberg, R. J. "Parental Beliefs and Children's School Performance." *Child Development*, 1993, *64*, 36–56.

Perkins, D. N. *Smart Schools.* New York: Free Press, 1995.

Piaget, J. *The Origins of Intelligence in Children.* Madison, Conn.: International Universities Press, 1952.

Quinn, N., and Holland, D. "Introduction." In D. Holland and N. Quinn (eds.), *Cultural Models in Language and Thought.* Cambridge, England: Cambridge University Press, 1987.

Rosch, E. "Cognitive Representations of Semantic Categories." *Journal of Experimental Psychology: General*, 1975, *104*, 192–233.

Russell, B. *A History of Western Philosophy.* New York: Simon & Schuster, 1945.

Salili, F., Maehr, M. L., and Gillmore, G. L. "Achievement and Morality: A Cross-Cultural Analysis of Causal Attribution and Evaluation." *Journal of Personality and Social Psychology*, 1976, *33*, 327–337.

Salili, F., and Mak, P.H.T. "Subjective Meaning of Success in High and Low Achievers." *International Journal of Intercultural Relations*, 1988, *12*, 125–138.

Scheffler, I. *Conditions of Knowledge: An Introduction to Epistemology and Education.* Chicago: University of Chicago Press, 1965.

Serpell, R. *The Significance of Schooling: Life Journeys in an African Society.* Cambridge, England: Cambridge University Press, 1993.

Shaver, P., Schwartz, J., Kirson, D., and O'Connor, C. "Emotion Knowledge: Further Exploration of a Prototype Approach." *Journal of Personality and Social Psychology*, 1987, *52*, 1061–1086.

Singleton, J. "Gambaru: A Japanese Cultural Theory of Learning." In J. Shields (ed.), *Japanese Schooling.* University Park: Pennsylvania State University Press, 1989.

Spiro, M. E. "Collective Representations and Mental Representations in Religious Symbol Systems." In B. Kilborne and L. L. Langness (eds.), *Culture and Human Nature.* Chicago: University of Chicago Press, 1987.

Sternberg, R. J. "Implicit Theories of Intelligence, Creativity, and Wisdom." *Journal of Personality and Social Psychology*, 1985, *49*, 607–627.

Stevenson, H. W., and Lee, S. Y. "Contexts of Achievement: A Study of American, Chinese, and Japanese Children." *Monographs of the Society for Research in Child Development*, 1990, *55* (1–2). Serial no. 221.

Stevenson, H. W., and Stigler, J. W. *The Learning Gap: Why Our Schools Are Failing and What We Can Learn from Japanese and Chinese Education.* New York: Simon & Schuster, 1992.

Strauss, C. "Models of Motives." In R. G. D'Andrade and C. Strauss (eds.), *Human Motives and Cultural Models*. Cambridge, England: Cambridge University Press, 1992.

Student Learning Orientation Group. *Why Do Students Learn? A Six-Country Study of Student Motivation*. Brighton, England: Institute of Development Studies, University of Sussex, 1987.

Suárez-Orozco, C., and Suárez-Orozco, M. *Transformations: Immigration, Family Life, and Achievement Motivation Among Latino Adolescents*. Stanford, Calif.: Stanford University Press, 1995.

Super, C. M. "Cultural Variation in the Meaning and Uses of Children's Intelligence." In J. B. Deregowski, S. Dziurawiec, and R. C. Annis (eds.), *Expiscations in Cross-Cultural Psychology*. Lisse, Netherlands: Swets and Zeitlinger, 1983.

Tu, W. M. *Humanity and Self-Cultivation: Essays in Confucian Thought*. Berkeley, Calif.: Asian Humanities Press, 1979.

Varenne, H., and McDermott, R. *Successful Failure: The School America Builds*. Boulder, Colo.: Westview Press, 1998.

Vernon, P. E. *Intelligence and Cultural Environment*. London: Methuen, 1969.

Wang, H., and others. *Xiandai Hanyu Pinlu Cidian* [Dictionary of the frequency of vocabulary in modern Chinese]. Beijing, China: Beijing Languages Institute Press, 1986.

Weiner, B. *An Attributional Theory of Motivation and Emotion*. New York: Springer-Verlag, 1986.

Wentzel, K. R., and Caldwell, K. "Friendships, Peer Acceptance, and Group Membership: Relations to Academic Achievement in Middle School." *Child Development*, 1997, 68, 1198–1209.

White, M. *The Japanese Educational Challenge*. New York: Free Press, 1987.

White, M., and LeVine, R. "What Is an 'ii ko' (Good Child)?" In H. Stevenson, H. Azuma, and K. Hakuta (eds.), *Child Development in Japan*. New York: Freeman, 1987.

Wober, M. "Towards an Understanding of the Kiganda Concept of Intelligence." In J. W. Berry and P. R. Dasen (eds.), *Culture and Cognition*. London: Methuen, 1974.

Wu, S.-P., and Lai, C.-Y. *Complete Text of the Four Books and Five Classics in Modern Chinese*. Beijing, China: International Culture Press, 1992. (In Chinese.)

Yang, J. *Hsun Tzu*. Shanghai, China: Ancient Books Publishing House, 1979.

Yang, S.-Y., and Sternberg, R. J. "Taiwanese Chinese People's Conceptions of Intelligence." *Intelligence*, 1997, 25, 21–29.

Yu, A.-B. "Ultimate Life Concerns, Self, and Chinese Achievement Motivation." In M. Bond (ed.), *The Handbook of Chinese Psychology*. New York: Oxford University Press, 1996.

JIN LI is assistant professor of education and human development at Brown University, Providence, Rhode Island.

Cross-cultural study of motivation to learn in school suggests that many constructs may not generalize across cultures. Culturally sensitive, multimethod approaches that can research meaning making may increase understanding of motivation in context.

Achievement Motivation Across Cultures: Some Puzzles and Their Implications for Future Research

Neil Hufton, Julian G. Elliott, Leonid Illushin

Our comparative research into academic motivation in Kentucky, Sunderland (in the United Kingdom), and St. Petersburg in Russia has thrown up a number of puzzles with interesting and perhaps wide-ranging implications for existing theory and future research and theorization. We begin with a discussion of how two puzzling findings from our own and others' research might relate to current theory, but wonder whether they might just reflect the inquiry methods that generated them. We then consider possible applications of theory to our research in Russia and raise a deeper question as to whether some current theory aptly applies to learning in school contexts anywhere. We conclude with some suggestions for forms of research that might help to reduce the occurrence of avoidable puzzles and offer the possibility of a transcultural approach to motivational research.

The two puzzling findings concern the relation between self-perception of academic competence and achievement and attribution of achievement to effort or ability:

- Positive academic self-perception appears to correlate positively with achievement within national cohorts but negatively when cohorts are compared between countries (compare Shen and Pedulla, 2000).
- American and English adolescents were more likely to attribute high achievement to effort than to ability, although they made significantly less effort than did Russian adolescents, who were more likely to attribute high achievement to ability than to effort.

Self-Perception of Academic Competence and Achievement

One way to explain how positive academic self-perception might correlate positively with achievement within a national cohort but not in between-country comparisons would be to suggest that American and English children feel unwarrantedly positive about their academic competence and effectively overvalue their achievement (Rosenberg, 1979; Wylie, 1979). Several studies, including our own, appear to support this notion. Although American students perform poorly compared with students in Japan and China, they thought that they did well in mathematics and science and were more likely to rate these subjects as easy (Stevenson and Stigler, 1992; Becker, Sawada, and Shimizu, 1999). In a six-nation comparative study (Krauthammer, 1990), American children scored lowest on a standardized mathematics test yet were the most positive about themselves. Thus, 68 percent of the American children, as against only 23 percent of Korean children, the nation that scored highest on the test, agreed with the statement, "I am good at mathematics." Similarly, in an analysis of data from the Third International Mathematics and Science Study (TIMSS), Keys, Harris, and Fernandes (1997) found that 93 percent of the English and 86 percent of the U.S. students agreed that they were doing well in mathematics, compared with the significantly higher-achieving students from Singapore (57 percent) and Japan (44 percent).

Such differences are not confined to comparisons with Asian countries. Although exhibiting superior performance in mathematics, fewer students in both France and Germany saw themselves in as positive a light as the American or English cohorts (Beaton and others, 1996). Another study, this one comparing English with Danish and French students (Osborn, 1999), reported that the English were least likely to evaluate succeeding in school as difficult. Other research has found that North American children tend to have more positive self-perceptions than do their peers in China (Kwok and Lytton, 1996), Germany (Schneider, Borkowski, Kurtz, and Kerwin, 1986; Oettingen, 1995), and Russia (Oettingen, 1995).

Our own research seems to bear out these findings. In a series of studies, we have surveyed the self-perceptions of more than six thousand students aged nine to ten and fourteen to fifteen years, together with the perceptions of their teachers and parents, and held interviews with 144 students and 130 teachers in Kentucky, Sunderland, and St. Petersburg.

When we asked students to indicate whether they thought they were "very good," "good," "average," "not very good," or "poor" at schoolwork (Elliott, Hufton, Hildreth, and Illushin, 1999; Elliott, Hufton, Illushin, and Lauchlan, 2001), we got very different answers from the various cohorts. In St. Petersburg, more children perceived themselves as below than above average. In contrast, the Kentucky and Sunderland children reported very positive self-appraisals, with only a small proportion seeing themselves as below average. Similar between-country trends were found for student self-satisfaction with current educational achievements, work rate, and capacity for improvement. When students were asked what they considered their parents thought of their abilities, Sunderland and Kentucky students were considerably more likely to perceive their parents as having a more positive view of them than they had of themselves. Such a trend was much less marked among the St. Petersburg students.

In our sample of more than three thousand parents (Elliott, Hufton, Illushin, and Willis, 2001), only 14 percent of respondents in St. Petersburg thought their children were above average, compared with 65 percent in Kentucky and 71 percent in Sunderland. In St. Petersburg, only 52 percent, but in Kentucky 75 percent and in Sunderland 81 percent, were satisfied with their children's educational attainments. A greater proportion of St. Petersburg parents believed that their children could improve their performance significantly.

To evaluate the effect of teacher messages on student self-perceptions (Entwistle, Alexander, Pallas, and Cadigan, 1987; Murdock, 1999), we asked the nine and ten year olds (Elliott, Hufton, Illushin, and Lauchlan, 2001) to rate how they thought their class teacher perceived them and asked their teachers to rate each of the children, with both groups using the same scale. Sixty-eight percent of the American sample believed that their teachers thought them to be "very good" or "quite good"; in actuality, only 50 percent of the teachers had so rated them. In Sunderland, the students' overestimate was even greater (60 percent and 39 percent, respectively). In St. Petersburg, children not only underestimated their teachers' perceptions of them (26 percent and 52 percent), but twice as many children (30 percent) thought that their teachers would see them as "below average" than was actually the case (15 percent).

There are several possible explanations of these differences. As already noted, it is possible that the very high perceptions of the English and American students result from a relatively undemanding educational system where very high levels of student engagement are more rarely observed (Goodlad, 1984; Steinberg, 1996). In line with this thinking, Kawanaka, Stigler, and Hiebert (1999) have argued that the positive perceptions of American children may be related to relatively undemanding curricular demands. Using TIMSS videotaped studies of grade 8 mathematics teaching in the United States, Japan, and Germany, the mathematics content in the American classrooms was adjudged to be lower than in Germany and Japan. Self-perceptions were inversely related to the difficulty of the material and the TIMSS scores in the three countries. This, these authors contend, is suggestive of a clear link among task demands, self-perceptions, and actual performance.

A further closely related factor may be the strong premium placed on the belief that students need to feel good about themselves and their achievements. It is commonly accepted in both England and the United States that having a positive self-perception may foster striving to achieve in all aspects of life, and perhaps especially in education, where research has suggested that students' belief in their academic capability strongly influences their motivation and performance in school (Martin and Debus, 1998; Vrugt, 1994; McInerney, Roche, McInerney, and Marsh, 1997; Marsh and Yeung, 1997). Teachers and clinicians have observed the demotivating and alienating impact of a diminished sense of self-efficacy, competence, or esteem on students with learning difficulties (Pressley and McCormick, 1995). Their students' future engagement in learning seems crucially to depend on countering these negative influences. However, from what is almost certainly the case for many children with learning difficulties, teachers seem to have drawn the wider inference that raising self-esteem and achieving a very strong sense of competence are prerequisite for maximizing *all* students' learning. Such a perspective seems often to translate into a suppression of criticism and a maximization of praise in classroom encounters.

Other factors may have reinforced this tendency. In England during the 1980s, strong encouragement of teachers to stress the positive in managing classroom behavior (Wheldall and Merrett, 1985) resulted in changes in teacher behavior that appear to have persisted to the present (Harrop and Swinson, 2000). Alexander (2000) found English primary teachers so eager to be positive that they "ended up devaluing the evaluation to the point where its function was merely phatic" (p. 369). Broadfoot, Osborn, Gilly, and Bucher (1993) similarly found that English teachers were more uncritically praising than French teachers. In the United States, a tendency on the part of teachers to be critical (White, 1975) was overcome by the mid-1980s, and positive comments became more frequent than negative (Wyatt and Hawkins, 1987).

In addition to positive oral feedback, American students have long tended to receive very positive messages in the form of grades for personal work: "More than one mother shook her head over the fact that her daughter never does any studying at home and is out every evening but gets A's in all her work" (Lynd and Lynd, 1929, p. 195).

Concern was expressed in the U.S. governmental report *A Nation at Risk* (National Commission on Excellence in Education, 1983) about a steady inflation of grades unwarranted by actual achievement. Studies of college entrants have reported that steadily increasing school grades neither reflected the volume of study taking place outside school (Sykes, 1995; Ziomek and Svec, 1997) nor were reflected in Scholastic Aptitude Test or American College Test scores (Sax, Astin, Korn, and Mahoney, 2000). In a comparative study, Ban and Cummings (1999) reported that American teachers awarded much higher grades to students and tended to offer praise far more frequently than Japanese teachers did. Sykes (1995) went so far as to argue that grades no longer accurately reflected academic performance; rather, "content-free 'A's have become tools of affirmation, therapy and public relations" (p. 31).

By contrast, although the St. Petersburg teachers in interviews recognized a role for praise in motivating students (Hufton, Elliott, and Illushin, 2002b), our observations of classroom practice suggest that praise was employed much more sparingly than in the United States or Britain. Both Alexander (2000) and Muckle (1988, 1990) noted that Russian teachers tend to be more critical and challenging than English or American teachers. Alexander cited a Russian informant who wryly commented that unlike the culture in American schools, exemplified by the poster "100 Ways to Praise a Child," there were only a handful of praise descriptors in Russian, while "the vocabulary of disapproval is rich and varied" (Alexander, 2000, p. 375).

A number of conclusions have been drawn from these various findings. Drawing on TIMMS data, Shen and Pedulla (2000) found that children in higher-scoring countries tended to have lower self-perceptions of academic competence. Such findings raise the question as to whether excessive use of praise may lead individuals to underestimate what is involved in securing worthwhile longer-term achievements (Lundeberg, Fox, Brown, and Elbedour, 2000) and develop an exaggerated sense of their abilities and a depreciation of adult evaluations (Stevenson, Chen, and Uttal, 1990; Stevenson and Stigler, 1992; Damon, 1995). Stevenson and his colleagues (Stevenson, Chen, and Uttal, 1990; Stevenson and Stigler, 1992) have argued strongly that unduly positive estimations of children's abilities, together with low expectations, have had a negative impact on American children's academic performance.

Others have argued that maintaining a positive conception of self is a functional requirement in American, and to a lesser extent English, society (Campbell, 1986; Marks, 1984; Seligman, 1995). Baumeister, Tice, and Hutton (1989) have suggested that Americans possess a largely positive view of themselves, and Greenberg and Pyszczynski (1985) and Blaine and Crocker (1993) have argued that it is important to Americans to maintain and enhance that self-perception. Heine, Lehman, Markus, and Kitayama (1999) contend that accentuating a sense of competence is critical for Americans in reducing any dissonance that might arise between cultural ideals of self-contained individuality and realistic self-appraisal. This may be less necessary in cultures where self-contained individuality is less valued or its maintenance makes more relaxed, or narrower, demands in terms of competence.

Explanations in terms of wider cultural climates are inevitably interesting and may have prima facie plausibility. It is, however, difficult to establish whether such climates, and the range of their potential effects, have been fully identified and correctly characterized and whether and how climates reliably generate observed individual effects. Furthermore, on the basis of research to date, we cannot yet conclude that the puzzling finding— that positive academic self-perception appears to correlate with achievement within national cohorts, but not when cohorts are compared between countries—is not, in part, an artifact of the research design that generated it.

Although in-depth interviews with students (Hufton, Elliott, and Illushin, 2002a) produced strong evidence that supported our earlier findings that the St. Petersburg students worked much harder yet were less satisfied with their performance and work rate, we are still left with doubts about our respondents' differing construals of the concepts under investigation. It would be possible for differences between the countries to be accounted for in part by a mismatch between meanings attributed to items, on what were mistakenly considered to function as common scales for quantifying degrees of either achievement or academic self-perception across cultures. Our qualitative findings suggest that academic self-perception relates to different or dissimilarly valued notions of education between cultures. Equally, although achievement may be objectified as a score on a TIMSS test, it seems that students are normally more likely, as Shen and Pedulla (2000) imply, to relate their sense of achievement to some accommodation of the intellectual demands of tasks, the role and definition of education in their locale, the normative responses of peers, the expectations of parents, and feedback from teachers. We will return to the many questions raised by attempts to scale the value of variables cross-culturally.

Ability and Effort

Our second puzzling finding was that American and English adolescents were more likely to attribute high achievement to effort than to ability, though they appeared to make significantly less effort than did Russian adolescents, who were more likely to attribute high achievement to ability than to effort.

It has recently been argued that students' tendency to attribute achievement to ability rather than to effort is a significant explanatory factor for the poorer performance of U.S. (Stevenson, Lee, and Stigler, 1986; Stevenson and Stigler, 1992) and English (Gipps, 1996; Reynolds and Farrell, 1996) students in comparison to their peers in Asian societies, where effort is seen as virtuous and praiseworthy. Attributional theory (Weiner, 1979) suggests that the belief that one has a fixed endowment of ability—beyond one's control—is likely to reduce the motivation to work hard, particularly at tasks estimated to carry a significant risk of failure. In contrast, if effort is seen as most important in determining outcomes, potential failure can be overcome by making greater effort. Stevenson and Stigler (1992) have argued that American education is unlikely to be improved until people can "change their self-defeating beliefs about the limits that innate ability places on achievement" (p. 112).

Initially persuaded by this view, we asked our student sample (Elliott, Hufton, Illushin, and Lauchlan, 2001; Elliott, Hufton, Hildreth, and Illushin, 1999) to rank the relative importance of ability and effort in securing achievement. Our data, both quantitative and observational, suggested that of the three groups, the St. Petersburg students were much more highly academically engaged in terms of both on-task activity in class and study time at home. We were therefore surprised that they emphasized effort less than the Kentucky or Sunderland students did. In particular, the older Russian students (those fourteen and fifteen years old) tended to prioritize ability. Equally surprising was the very strong emphasis of the Kentucky and Sunderland cohorts on effort. Similar trends were found in our parent study. In St. Petersburg, 54 percent of parents attributed achievement in school to effort and 28 percent to ability. In Kentucky, the respective ratios were 68 percent and 16 percent, and in Sunderland 78 percent and 11 percent (Elliott, Hufton, Illushin, and Willis, 2001). When asked what was important for their children to gain well-paid employment, Kentucky and Sunderland parents placed hard work before ability; the St. Petersburg parents disagreed.

Other investigators have queried whether the apparent Western emphasis on ability attributions and their supposed impact on motivation is wholly valid (Gipps and Tunstall, 1998; Chaplain, 2000). Bempechat and Drago-Severson (1999) pointed to findings from TIMSS (Beaton and others, 1996) indicating that in comparison with students from such high-scoring countries as Singapore, Japan, and Korea, American (and also English) adolescents tended to place greater emphasis on the importance of hard work and played down the role of natural ability. In the TIMSS follow-up study (Martin and others, 2000), a survey of teachers indicated that American informants were far less likely than those in Russia, or to a lesser extent England, to agree with the statement that some students had a natural ability for science and others did not. In comparison with European children, other studies similarly indicate that American children are more likely to attribute academic outcomes to effort (Schneider, Borkowski, Kurtz, and Kerwin, 1986; Kurtz, Carr, and Schneider, 1988; Kurtz and others, 1988).

In a series of detailed one-on-one interviews with 144 fifteen year olds from the same schools used in our 1999 survey, the relative importance of effort over ability was again powerfully stressed by the Kentucky and Sunderland students (Hufton, Elliott, and Illushin, 2002a). Although such a view was also common among St. Petersburg youngsters, a significant number emphasized the need for talent in a particular subject if the very highest grades were to be awarded:

> I think that there are certain subjects that require some special ability or talent. For me, it's physics. Hard work here may not necessarily bring best results.
>
> If a person is talented, but doesn't work hard, he won't get good marks, not the best ones, because he may not do his homework and come to school thinking he can get everything at the lesson. And sometimes he may be able to do this, but he'll get a good, not the best mark. And if a person who is not very talented sees the task and thinks, "This is very difficult for me", so, he'll come home and work hard for the whole day. If he comes to school the next

day, he will get a good mark too. And if a very talented person works hard, only in this case, he will get an excellent mark.

The Kentucky students, in contrast, were considerably more likely to highlight the role of effort in achieving good grades: "You can reach your goals if you work hard at them. So, like, if your goal is to be in Harvard, you can work toward your goal and get into Harvard. It might take a little longer than it would for others, but you can still get to the top."

Kentucky students, in particular, implied that teachers might grade as much on effort as on achievement: "I think [teachers] count effort more here than anything. They just want you to try your best, and they give you a good grade just for trying as hard as you can."

As we explored student accounts of the use of their time and observed practices in school, we came to two important realizations:

- Valuing effort and deploying effort need not correlate, and both valuation and deployment may be complexly influenced by peer and community norms in each culture.
- Meanings attributed to such terms as *effort* and *ability* may vary within a culture and between cultures.

A belief in the importance of effort need not generate actual high work rates. In our research, although American and English children very clearly emphasize effort, the volume and quality of academic engagement was significantly less than that in St. Petersburg. There, students who thought that it was talent that counts nonetheless normally and habitually put in a great deal more working time in lessons and for homework over a longer school day and week (Elliott, Hufton, Hildreth, and Illushin, 1999; Elliott, Hufton, Illushin, and Lauchlan, 2001; Elliott, Hufton, Illushin, and Willis, 2001; Hufton, Elliott, and Illushin, 2002a; Alexander, 2000).

Against local norms, our Kentucky respondents thought they were working hard. Thus, within their perceptions, there was little contradiction between their endorsement of the value of hard work in school and their actual lifestyles. It was not that our American informants were idle. Many reported involvement in team sports and a wide range of recreational, social, and religious activities. Adolescent sleep deficit was reported as a concern for teachers and parents. However, it was not incurred through meeting academic demands. Indeed, permitting homework to be undertaken during class time (a frequently observed practice in the United States: Stevenson and Nerison-Low, 1998; Martin and others, 2000) seemed likely to reinforce students' belief that adequate effort was being made, as would the reported achievement of high grades in school, with little homework.

By contrast, much more demanding work rates appeared to be normative in St. Petersburg. Indeed, Russian commentators (Baranov, 1998; Fillippov, 2000) have expressed alarm about the high levels of stress and fatigue resulting from the demands of schooling. Russian schooling is formulated to move students together through a progressively demanding curriculum (Hufton and Elliott, 2000). Students asserted that they would be unable to cope with lessons without several hours of independent study each evening. It was in this context that Russian teenagers observed that hard work alone was often insufficient to achieve the highest grades and that some definite talent for a subject was necessary (Hufton, in press). That is, ability emerged as the finally discriminating variable, where high levels of academic effort could be taken for granted (Alexander, 2000). In Kentucky, in contrast, a lesser curriculum demand, coupled with greater variation in viable levels of academic engagement, seemed likely to accentuate students' perception of effort as the discriminant variable.

Analysis of our student interview data tends to support Bempechat and Drago-Severson's (1999) warnings about the limitations of survey data and the dangers of reducing such complex terms as *effort* and *ability* to dichotomous constructs. As with self-perception and achievement, these findings may at least partly reflect the difficulty of operationalizing and measuring complex constructs cross-culturally.

Students' (and, indeed, parents' and teachers') ideas of ability seem to occupy differing folk psychological dimensions in each culture. In England, students contrasted being "intelligent" with being "thick" and in Kentucky, being "smart" with being "dumb." Our research data suggest that the American notion of "smart" refers to a facility that can be increased by effort: the harder you work, the smarter you can become. In England, however, intelligence tends to be seen as a more fixed attribute that is less amenable to change. In Russia, students tended to oppose "having a talent" for something (a subject) with not having a talent. Clearly, it should not be presupposed that these are just different ways of expressing ideas about an equivalent construct. As Pomerantz and Saxon (2001) have observed, differing conceptions may be related to a variety of different student attitudes, beliefs, and outcomes. Equally, with regard to the apparently simpler concept of effort, not only time but the nature of study tasks and the degree of concentration involved in study may well be important subvariables, finding differing values in different cultures. In the absence of a conceptual or semantic map of interrelations between these and other implicated terms for each culture, it is not clear how differences in the folk usages, necessarily deployed in instruments devised for native respondents, can be confidently related to culturally transcendent notions of ability and effort.

Problems of Fit Between Anglo-American Motivation Theory and Russian Schooling Practice

During the course of our research, a deeper puzzle also emerged. In facing the challenge to account for the generally high motivation of students in Russia, we found ourselves worryingly dependent on culture as an explanatory variable. In seeking to avoid a facile recourse to a protean factor, which can take on many convenient values, we were led further to query whether current Western theories of motivation might not account too well for motivation to learn in school in the West.

How did Russian schooling seem to problematize Western theory? On the face of it, Russian schooling, where students followed, lesson by lesson, a rather closely prescribed and intensive curriculum, might seem likely to involve teachers' use of extrinsic motivators. Furthermore, as Muckle (1990), Alexander (2000), and O'Brien (2000) have also noted, Russian teachers' motivational approach appears to tend more toward sanction than reward, with praise sparingly given and corrective feedback frequent, so that self-esteem and the sense of self-efficacy and, as a result, future motivation might be predicted to be thereby reduced. However, most students seemed to maintain, and many reported a relative increase in, self-directed motivation as they progressed through schooling into adolescence. Teachers' motivational approaches did not seem to undermine the development of high student levels of engagement. Nor did the effects of what presented to us as sanctions seem to become blunted through familiarity. However, as Ryan and Deci (2000) have pointed out, there are various forms of extrinsic motivation, which can differ in the degree to which they demonstrate elements of autonomy. They differentiate among externally imposed and reinforced forms of regulation, internal regulation prompted by the need to avoid guilt or shame and achieve a sense of pride and sense of worth, and more autonomous forms of extrinsic motivation, where the individual identifies with the personal importance of specific behaviors and perceives them as congruent with their wider value system. Although behavior in this latter circumstance is more volitional and valued by the individual, it remains extrinsic because it is undertaken for an instrumental outcome rather than as an end in itself. Here there appears to be strong resonance with our observations in Russian classrooms.

Second, although our secondary school St. Petersburg students attributed academic success significantly more to ability than to effort, they made significant and sustained effort.

Third, although seeing learning as constantly demanding, with success uncertain, the St. Petersburg students' sense of self-efficacy—that they could achieve with effort—seemed mostly strong.

Fourth, in terms of expectancy theory (Eccles, 1983; Eccles and Wigfield, 1995), the St. Petersburg students seemed more to "travel hopefully," with a faith in the anticipated utility of effort, than to be influenced by expectations of their final level of success. Although there was some evidence of students' beginning to evaluate the importance and utility of particular tasks and subjects in relation to hoped-for careers, the more central impression was of students' accepting tasks as valuable because they were seen as contributing to becoming educated, itself highly valued. There was little in our evidence to suggest that they construed the value of tasks in terms of the interest (intrinsic value), future usefulness (utility value), or cost value of the task (Eccles, 1983). Although interest was reported as making tasks more enjoyable or easier, it did not seem to lead students to direct effort to the interesting at the expense of the less interesting. That the costs of learning might vary among students and, for individuals, among subjects was recognized, but that they had to be met in terms of the commitment of effort was taken for granted, even among the few who in practice balked at the costs.

Fifth, there was strong evidence of students' pursuing mastery goals and making significant effort to secure learning and improvement for their intrinsic value—as a means of personal growth. However, the selection of mastery goals seemed significantly more dominated by the expectations of the prescribed curriculum than by personal choice. There was little evidence to suggest that any student was much motivated by the desire to succeed relative to peers (that is, by performance-approach goals), though strong peer allegiance to classmates may have inhibited the expression of such goals. A number of students were clearly motivated by the desire to play an adequate part in a largely learning-oriented class and stand in good stead in the eyes of their teacher. It seemed important to avoid peers' and teachers' perception of one as an uncommitted or uncooperative student. Perhaps these were Russian equivalents to "performance-avoid" goals (Dweck and Leggett, 1988), but if so, they lacked any connotation of refraining from performance to avoid looking "stupid." On the contrary, it was not unusual for students who did not understand something to request to work in front of the class on the blackboard, so that teacher and peers could follow and correct their working.

Finally, St. Petersburg schools seem to achieve effective and sustained levels of motivation in their students without fulfilling many of the motivation-theory-derived prescriptions informing several current American programs to improve instructional practice. Yair (2000) has summarized these approvingly as involving authenticity of learning tasks, student choice of learning task, student autonomy as to modes of tackling tasks, student agency in undertaking tasks, and a requirement to develop high-level skills in the course of completing a task.

Authenticity is a slippery concept. In Yair's usage, its meaning seems to range from "real-life" learning "in environments [children] know, and that have importance for their immediate and long-term life goals" (p. 195), to the possibly rather different "focusing on important, universal and personally challenging issues" (p. 195), to involving the more modest "instruction [which is] more relevant (and . . . diverse)" (p. 206). While U.S. studies (such as Marks, 2000) suggest that authentic activities are more likely to be associated with higher levels of engagement, we would doubt on the basis of our evidence that authenticity, in the sense of learning from actual or closely simulated real-life situations, characterizes much of Russian students' learning in school. We have good intimations, however, that wherever subject matter lends itself, there has been a sustained and high-level statewide attempt to identify what are thought to be important and universal issues with the potential to be personally (because humanly) challenging and to develop, try out, and refine centrally approved instructional materials and processes. If the resultant programs and textbooks articulate a form of authenticity, then it is the archetypal or paradigmatic authenticity of the instructive story, case, or example, aiming to address students' existential, rather than the contingent and material, immediacy, which seems implied in the Western prescriptions.

Equally, St. Petersburg students had very little choice of learning task—perhaps only between, for example, easier and harder variants of mathematics problems—and autonomy and agency were restricted to any personal ways students might have developed for going about prescribed study and learning. It seemed that students were expected to develop progressively higher-level intellectual and metacognitive skills, which instruction aimed to model and foster, but as we have suggested elsewhere (Hufton and Elliott, 2000), the pressure to develop these appeared to arise through the demand of a more immediate requirement for memorization, which as Marton, Watkins, and Tang (1997), Gow, Balla, Kember, and Tai Hau (1995) and Biggs (1994) have suggested, at least for Chinese students, can lead to higher-order learning.

Culture as an Explanatory Variable

We could account for these findings by making certain cultural postulates, for which there is at least reasonable evidence from our investigations and in the literature:

- That education is so highly valued for itself among Russians that children are socialized and enculturated from the earliest years to be strongly motivated to acquire it
- That the definition of *education* in Russia fully includes at least all that is taught in school
- That teachers, far from seen as imposing education on students, are perceived as necessary guides and supporters—and classmates as collaborators rather than competitors—in aiming at desired goals
- That student assessment rewards successful memorization, which responds to effort almost as much as understanding, which requires relevant abilities, until quite late in a student's school career

On these postulates, we could construct the following explanatory narrative. As a result of pervasive cultural influences, Russian students are so strongly motivated that they construe teacher correction as help and value it throughout their schooling. Because education is valued in itself, maturing students increasingly aim to achieve mastery goals rather than performance-approach goals. Performance-avoid goals are influential but take the form of a sufficient commitment to adequate performance, because poor performance threatens to undermine solidarity with collaborative peers and could present as ingratitude to helpful teachers. Because education is defined by the school curriculum, to which teachers are the best guides, students feel little need to value choice of learning task or autonomy in tackling tasks, especially where prescribed instructional tasks may be felt to be authentic. Although ability is finally decisive in securing the best grades, effort applied to successful memorization is sufficiently rewarded for students to maintain a sense of self-efficacy in proportion to their readiness to expend that effort throughout most of their schooling. There is little scope for the effects of other than very short-term expectancy on motivation, where learning involves steady, guided, and measured steps, along a generally valued, prescribed path, and where it is accepted that the cost will be the necessary effort. Student agency finds (a narrow but real) play in the development of increasingly effective study, learning, and metacognitive skills.

Motivation in the Context of Schooling

Concern that the culturally high value that Russians set on education should not be asked to do as much work as falls its way in the explanation above coincided with preliminary theorizing about schooling-related factors that might partially account for Russian students' motivation. We noted that Anglo American studies of motivation were not always strongly focused toward the longitudinal experience of learning through schooling. This seemed to reflect the origins of interest in the field of motivation: on the one hand, in correlates of demotivation among significantly behaviorally problematic and low-attaining students in school, and, on the other, in attributes of occasions of high motivation, among people generally, in any learning context. From the first group, study findings appeared to warrant the inference that raising self-esteem would raise motivation. From the second group of studies, it has been argued (Yair, 2000; Seifert and O'Keefe, 2001) that for instructional tasks to bring about motivation, they should consistently exhibit authenticity, choice, agency, autonomy, and the opportunity to acquire higher-order skills.

We do not question that poor self-esteem will be commonly associated with poor motivation or that authenticity, choice, agency, autonomy, and the opportunity to acquire higher-order skills often accompany high motivation. It is the relatively unresearched application of psychological findings to general instructional practice in publicly funded schools that may be problematic. It seems strongly possible to us that motivation theorists, through a research focus on individual motivation to complete decontextualized tasks, have allowed too little weight to two arguably inalienable features of learning through schooling.

The first feature is that teachers may engage with students as members of a class, or a smaller group, or one-on-one. However, the more time that is spent one-on-one, the less time can be given to each interaction.

Perversely, then, although one-on-one interaction should increase the quality of engagement with an individual's learning, in practice, there may often be too little time to appraise the student's learning condition and envisage and communicate an apt intervention. Where the most ambitious students choose highly diverse learning tasks, appraisal and intervention may prove beyond the unprepared competence of any particular teacher, at any apposite time for the student. As a result, proposals to increase motivation by the sort of radical individuation of learning tasks advocated by Yair (2000) risk falling foul of teachers' loss of information about, and so confidence in, and the ability to guarantee, the quality, value, and potential of consequent learning.

The second feature is that although education systems vary in the completeness and rigidity with which they prescribe curricula, schools are commonly under some requirement to engage students in at least some learning that they might not have chosen, that may not be of immediate interest, in sequences that do not make prior sense to them, at learning rates that a significant percentage of students find demanding. The more completely and rigidly curricula are prescribed (whether explicitly, or through the demands of high-stakes assessment), the more likely this is to be the case.

Given both of these circumstances, we doubt that motivating most students to learn in school can normally be expected, or must regularly need, to fulfill the conditions thought necessary to bring about the highest motivation. As a result, what schools and teachers may increasingly need to know is how they can sufficiently motivate the greatest number of learners to learn sufficiently in relation to a prescribed curriculum.

Situational Interest and Schooling

Hidi and Harackiewicz (2000) discuss some recent developments in motivation theory with strong relevance for contemporary schooling. While acknowledging the significance of individual interest, intrinsic motivation, and mastery goals for motivation to learn in school, they raise the question as to whether "the reluctance to recognise the potential additional benefits of external interventions, situational interest and performance goals" (p. 167) risks depriving educators of some important means of motivating children who do not "have interests that are easily adaptable to school settings and academic learning" (p. 157). They note a distinction in the literature between individual interest and situational interest. Although individual interest can generate powerful motivation and its origins in personal experience can sometimes be surmised, little is known about how to inculcate or nurture it. By contrast, situational interest is elicited by conditions or stimuli in the environment that focus attention and generate affect. They suggest that if situational interest could be sustained over time, knowledge, value, and positive affect might be expected to develop.

Early research suggested that situational interest could cause learners to focus attention, narrow inferences, and integrate new information with prior knowledge (Schank, 1979). More recent work has looked at text-stimulated situational interest and has found that ease of comprehension, novelty, surprise, vividness, intensity, character identification, and reading for a purpose increase interest and produce superior comprehension and recall (Benton and others, 1995; Schraw, Bruning, and Svoboda, 1995; Wade, Buxton, and Kelly, 1999). Equally, where instructional materials and processes evoke meaningful contexts and require more useful or personally relevant learning, situational interest may be engaged (Cordova and Lepper, 1996). Working in the presence of others may also increase situational interest (Isaac, Sansone, and Smith, 1999).

Hidi and Harackiewicz (2000) also note that students can generate and use strategies, including gamelike activities, to make boring tasks more interesting (Sansone, Wiebe, and Morgan, 1999). Faced with important or required tasks, they can control effort and maintain interest (Wolters, 1998). They argue that it would be valuable to know how teachers could foster the development of these responses to learning tasks.

A key problem for the potential role of situational, as compared to individual, interest lies in its instability and evanescence (Schraw and Lehman, 2001). Interest aroused in or by a situation can be "caught" but may not be "held" (Hidi and Baird, 1986). What educators would profit from knowing is how situational interest could be sufficiently aptly generated and sustained to create the possibility of at least valuable and, better still, cognitively and affectively meaningful learning for individuals. In effect, they need to know how to compose those constellations, or blends, of situational motivators that most promote the engagement of sufficient individual interest to bring about an adequate measure of intrinsic motivation, itself a construct conceived of differently by various U.S. researchers (Murphy and Alexander, 2000).

Hidi and Harackiewicz (2000) argue that researching such constellations may involve the recontextualization of some previous work on extrinsic motivation, which has suggested that "tangible rewards undermined intrinsic motivation" (p. 158). They argue that such research has tended to focus on "relatively short-term and relatively simple activities" (p. 159), where both activities and rewards were decontextualized. Such research may fail to throw light on the combined role of sets, or sequences of rewards, in stimulating initial situational interest or in aptly (re)invigorating long-term, complex, and effortful engagements, where "dependence on external feedback continues throughout development" (p. 168). Hidi and Harackiewicz conclude that "a combination of carefully administered external rewards and situationally interesting activities may be one of the most realistic approaches to educational intervention" (p. 159).

Our Russian findings resonate quite strongly with many aspects of Hidi and Harackiewicz's discussion. We have elsewhere (Hufton and Elliott, 2000) described what we termed a pedagogical nexus that could bear redescription as a constellation or blend of sustained situational motivators that seemed to promote the development of sufficient individual interest to engage intrinsic motivation. We suggested that the Russian textbook acted as "a repertoire of pedagogical paradigms" maximizing "curriculum meaningfulness" for pupils (p. 121). We recognized the significant role of working collectively with fellow students in sustaining situational interest. We noted that notwithstanding the frequency of whole-class teaching in Russian schools, its conduct, and particularly the manner of oral review, fulfilled the function of providing students with frequent unthreatening feedback on their learning. Assessment functioned, along with other forms of valued recognition, to reward effort as well as ability. Interviews with students suggested that many of them had devised strategies for study, when, at least initially, they were not strongly motivated by interest. Furthermore, a number of them reported becoming interested as a consequence of such study.

Conclusion

Thus far, our Russian findings no more than resonate with Hidi and Harackiewicz's discussion. We conclude by considering what kinds of research might best test the validity of such apparent resonance.

First, as is clear from our discussion of our puzzling findings, we see attempts to compare motivation in different cultures by reference to supposedly culture-free or neutral scales, or instruments, as premature. Consequently, we see no alternative but to explore relations between motivationally relevant folk psychological terms in each culture of interest as preliminary to attempting to understand relations between the resulting conceptual maps.

Second, we think that it is important that studies of motivation to learn in school explore the possibility that it might be substantially procured by the persistent administration of "a combination of carefully administered external rewards and situationally interesting activities" (Hidi and Harackiewicz, 2000, p. 168). If that is the case, rather than attempting to infer the nature of such combinations from decontextualized theory, we need new studies that attempt to surface general features of their character and operation in naturalistic contexts.

These two approaches should also enable some better appreciation of the otherwise amorphous and indeterminate influence of culture. Motivationally relevant folk psychological terms stand at an interface between the wider culture and the management of motivation in schools. If we had a better understanding of their uses in the contexts of schooling practice, it would simultaneously illuminate actual and effective linkages between wider cultural beliefs and educational motives, actions, and behaviors. At the same time, cross-cultural studies of motivation to learn in school may help to establish whether the dominant explanatory variables are owed to cultural variance or whether schooling is a sufficiently autonomous institution for common schooling variables to be intermapped, across cultures. As Bempechat and Drago-Severson (1999) have argued, it is time for a qualitative turn in the cross-cultural study of motivation.

References

Alexander, R. J. *Culture and Pedagogy: International Comparisons in Primary Education.* Cambridge, Mass.: Blackwell, 2000.

Ban, T., and Cummings, W. K. "Moral Orientations of Schoolchildren in the United States and Japan." *Comparative Education Review,* 1999, *43,* 64–85.

Baranov, A. "A Real Threat to the Nation's Future." *Russian Education and Society,* 1998, *40,* 6–16.

Baumeister, R. F., Tice, D. M., and Hutton, D. G. "Self-Presentational Motivations and Personality Differences in Self-Esteem." *Journal of Personality,* 1989, *57,* 547–579.

Beaton, A. E., and others. *Mathematics Achievement in the Middle School Years: IEA's Third International Mathematics and Science Study (TIMSS).* Boston: Center for the Study of Testing, Evaluation, and Educational Policy, Boston College, 1996.

Becker, J. P., Sawada, T., and Shimizu, Y. "Some Findings of the US-Japan Cross-Cultural Research on Students' Problem-Solving Behaviors." In G. Kaiser, E. Luna, and I. Huntley (eds.), *International Comparisons in Mathematics Education.* Bristol, Pa.: Falmer Press, 1999.

Bempechat, J., and Drago-Severson, E. "Cross-National Differences in Academic Achievement: Beyond Etic Conceptions of Children's Understandings." *Review of Educational Research,* 1999, *69,* 287–314.

Benton, S. L., and others. "Knowledge, Interest and Narrative Writing." *Journal of Educational Psychology,* 1995, *87,* 66–79.

Biggs, J. "What Are Effective Schools? Lessons from East and West." *Australian Educational Researcher,* 1994, *21,* 19–39.

Blaine, B., and Crocker, J. "Self-Esteem and Self-Serving Biases in Reaction to Positive and Negative Events: An Integrative Review." In R. Baumeister (ed.), *Self-Esteem: The Puzzle of Low Self-Regard.* New York: Plenum Press, 1993.

Broadfoot, P., Osborn, M., Gilly, M., and Bucher, A. *Perceptions of Teaching: Primary School Teachers in England and France.* London: Cassell, 1993.

Campbell, J. D. "Similarity and Uniqueness: The Effects of Attribute Type, Relevance and Individual Differences in Self-Esteem and Depression." *Journal of Personality and Social Psychology,* 1986, *50,* 281–294.

Chaplain, R. P. "Beyond Exam Results? Differences in the Social and Psychological Perceptions of Young Males and Females at School." *Educational Studies,* 2000, *26,* 177–190.

Cordova, D. I., and Lepper, M. R. "Intrinsic Motivation and the Process of Learning: Beneficial Effects of Contextualization, Personalization and Choice." *Journal of Educational Psychology,* 1996, *88,* 715–730.

Damon, W. *Greater Expectations.* New York: Free Press, 1995.

Dweck, C. S., and Leggett, E. L. "A Social-Cognitive Approach to Motivation and Personality." *Psychological Review,* 1988, *95,* 256–273.

Eccles, J. S. "Expectancies, Values and Academic Behaviors." In J. T. Spence (ed.), *Achievement and Achievement Motives.* New York: Freeman, 1983.

Eccles, J. S., and Wigfield, A. "In the Mind of the Actor: The Structure of Adolescents' Achievement Task Values and Expectancy-Related Beliefs." *Personality and Social Psychology Bulletin,* 1995, *21,* 215–225.

Elliott, J. G., Hufton, N., Anderman, E., and Illushin, L. "The Psychology of Motivation and Its Relevance to Educational Practice." *Educational and Child Psychology,* 2000, *17,* 121–137.

Elliott, J. G., Hufton, N., Hildreth, A., and Illushin, L. "Factors Influencing Educational

Motivation: A Study of Attitudes, Expectations and Behaviour of Children in Sunderland, Kentucky, and St. Petersburg." *British Educational Research Journal,* 1999, *25,* 75–94.

Elliott, J. G., Hufton, N., Illushin, L., and Lauchlan, F. "Motivation in the Junior Years: International Perspectives on Children's Attitudes, Expectations and Behaviour and Their Relationship to Educational Achievement." *Oxford Review of Education,* 2001, *27,* 37–68.

Elliott, J. G., Hufton, N., Illushin, L., and Willis, W. " 'The Kids Are Doing All Right': International Differences in Parental Satisfaction, Expectation and Attribution." *Cambridge Journal of Education,* 2001, *31,* 179–204.

Entwistle, D. R., Alexander, K. L., Pallas, A. M., and Cadigan, D. "The Emergent Academic Self-Image of First Graders: Its Response to Social Structure." *Child Development,* 1987, *58,* 1190–1206.

Fillippov, V. "On the Results of the Past Year and the Tasks of the Current Year." *Russian Education and Society,* 2000, *42,* 87–100.

Gipps, C. "The Paradox of the Pacific Rim Learner." *Times Educational Supplement,* Dec. 20, 1996, p. 13.

Gipps, C., and Tunstall, P. "Effort, Ability and the Teacher: Young Children's Explanations for Success and Failure." *Oxford Review of Education,* 1998, *24,* 149–165.

Goodlad, J. I. *A Place Called School: Prospects for the Future.* New York: McGraw-Hill, 1984.

Gow, L., Balla, J., Kember, D., and Tai Hau, K. "The Learning Approaches of Chinese People: A Function of Socialisation Processes and the Context of Learning?" In M. Bond (ed.), *Handbook of Chinese Psychology.* New York: Oxford University Press, 1995.

Greenberg, J., and Pyszczynski, T. "Compensatory Self-Inflation: A Response to the Threat to Self-Regard of Public Failure." *Journal of Personality and Social Psychology,* 1985, *49,* 273–280.

Harrop, A., and Swinson, J. "Natural Rates of Approval and Disapproval in British Infant, Junior and Secondary Classrooms." *British Journal of Educational Psychology,* 2000, *70,* 473–483.

Heine, S. J., Lehman, D. R., Markus, H. R., and Kitayama, S. "Is There a Universal Need for Positive Self-Regard?" *Psychological Review,* 1999, *106,* 766–794.

Hidi, S., and Baird, W. "Interestingness—A Neglected Variable in Discourse Processing." *Cognitive Science,* 1986, *10,* 179–194.

Hidi, S., and Harackiewicz, J. M. "Motivating the Academically Unmotivated: A Critical Issue for the 21st Century." *Review of Educational Research,* 2000, *70,* 151–179.

Hufton, N., and Elliott, J. G. "Motivation to Learn: The Pedagogical Nexus in the Russian School: Some Implications for Transnational Research and Policy Borrowing." *Educational Studies,* 2000, *26,* 115–136.

Hufton, N., Elliott, J. G., and Illushin, L. "Educational Motivation and Engagement: Qualitative Accounts from Three Countries." *British Educational Research Journal,* 2002a, *28*(2), 265–289.

Hufton, N., Elliott, J. G., and Illushin, L. "Teachers' Beliefs About Student Motivation: Similarities and Differences Across Cultures." Unpublished manuscript, 2002b.

Isaac, J., Sansone, C., and Smith, J. L. "Other People as a Source of Interest in an Activity." *Journal of Experimental Social Psychology,* 1999, *35,* 239–265.

Kawanaka, T., Stigler, J. W., and Hiebert, J. "Studying Mathematics Classrooms in Germany, Japan, and the United States: Lessons from the TIMSS Videotape Study." In G. Kaiser, E. Luna, and I. Huntley (eds.), *International Comparisons in Mathematics Education.* Bristol, Pa.: Falmer Press, 1999.

Keys, W., Harris, S., and Fernandes, C. *Third International Mathematics and Science Study, Second National Report, Part 2.* Slough, England: National Foundation for Educational Research, 1997.

Krauthammer, C. "Education: Doing Bad and Feeling Good." *Time,* Feb. 5, 1990, p. 78.

Kurtz, B. E., Carr, M., and Schneider, W. "Development of Attributional Beliefs and Self-Concept in German and American Children." Paper presented at the annual conference of the American Educational Research Association, New Orleans, Apr. 1988.

Kurtz, B. E., and others. "Sources of Memory and Metamemory Development: Societal, Parental and Educational Influences." In M. Gruneberg, P. Morris, and R. Sykes (eds.), *Proceedings of the Second International Conference on Practical Aspects of Memory.* New York: Wiley, 1988.

Kwok, D. C., and Lytton, H. "Perceptions of Mathematics Ability Versus Actual Mathematics Performance: Canadian and Hong Kong Chinese Children." *British Journal of Educational Psychology,* 1996, *66,* 209–222.

Lundeberg, M. A., Fox, P. W., Brown, A. C., and Elbedour, S. "Cultural Influences on Confidence: Country and Gender." *Journal of Educational Psychology,* 2000, *92,* 152–159.

Lynd, R., and Lynd, H. M. *Middletown: A Study in Modern American Culture.* New York: Harcourt, 1929.

Marks, G. "Thinking One's Abilities Are Unique and One's Opinions Are Common." *Personality and Social Psychology Bulletin,* 1984, *10,* 203–208.

Marks, H. M. "Student Engagement in Instructional Activity: Patterns in the Elementary, Middle and High School Years." *American Educational Research Journal,* 2000, *37,* 153–184.

Marsh, H. W., and Yeung, A. S. "Causal Effects of Academic Self-Concept on Academic Achievement: Structural Equation Models of Longitudinal Data." *Journal of Educational Psychology,* 1997, *89,* 41–54.

Martin, A. J., and Debus, R. L. "Self-Reports of Mathematics Self-Concept and Educational Outcomes: The Roles of Ego-Dimensions and Self-Consciousness." *British Journal of Educational Psychology,* 1998, *68,* 517–535.

Martin, M. O., and others. *TIMSS 1999: International Science Report.* Boston: International Study Center, Boston College, 2000.

Marton, F., Watkins, D., and Tang, C. "Discontinuities and Continuities in the Experience of Learning: An Interview Study of High-School Students in Hong Kong." *Learning and Instruction,* 1997, *7,* 21–48.

McInerney, D. M., Roche, L. A., McInerney, V., and Marsh, H. "Cultural Perspectives on School Motivation: The Relevance and Application of Goal Theory." *American Educational Research Journal,* 1997, *34,* 207–236.

Muckle, J. *A Guide to the Soviet Curriculum: What the Russian Child Is Taught in School.* London: Croom Helm, 1988.

Muckle, J. *Portrait of a Soviet School Under Glasnost.* Old Tappan, N.J.: Macmillan, 1990.

Murdock, T. N. "The Social Context of Risk: Status and Motivational Predictors of Alienation in Middle School." *Journal of Educational Psychology,* 1999, *91,* 62–75.

Murphy, P. K., and Alexander, P. A. "A Motivated Exploration of Motivation Terminology." *Contemporary Educational Psychology,* 2000, *25,* 3–53.

National Commission on Excellence in Education. *A Nation at Risk: The Imperative for Educational Reform.* Washington, D.C.: National Commission on Excellence in Education, 1983.

O'Brien, D. *From Moscow: Living and Teaching Among the Russians in the 1990s.* Nottingham, England: Bramcote Press, 2000.

Oettingen, G. "Cross-Cultural Perspectives on Self-Efficacy." In A. Bandura (ed.), *Self-Efficacy in Changing Societies.* Cambridge, England: Cambridge University Press, 1995.

Osborn, M. "Schooling and Learning in Three European Countries." *Compare,* 1999, *29,* 287–301.

Pomerantz, E. M., and Saxon, J. L. "Conceptions of Ability as Stable and Self-Evaluative Processes: A Longitudinal Examination." *Child Development,* 2001, *72,* 152–173.

Pressley, M., and McCormick, C. B. *Advanced Educational Psychology for Educators, Researchers and Policymakers.* New York: HarperCollins, 1995.

Reynolds, D., and Farrell, S. *Worlds Apart? A Review of International Surveys of Educational Achievement Involving England.* London: Her Majesty's Stationery Office, 1996.

Rosenberg, M. *Conceiving the Self.* New York: Basic Books, 1979.

Ryan, R. M., and Deci, D. L. "Intrinsic and Extrinsic Motivations: Classic Definitions and New Directions." *Contemporary Educational Psychology,* 2000, *25,* 54–67.

Sansone, C., Wiebe, D. J., and Morgan, C. "Self-Regulating Interest: The Moderating Role of Hardiness and Conscientiousness." *Journal of Personality,* 1999, *67,* 701–733.

Sax, L. J., Astin, A. W., Korn, W. S., and Mahoney, K. M. *The American Freshman: National Norms for Fall 2000.* Los Angeles: Higher Education Research Institute, University of California, 2000.

Schank, R. C. "Interestingness: Controlling Inferences." *Artificial Intelligence,* 1979, *12,* 273–297.

Schneider, W., Borkowski, J. G., Kurtz, B. E., and Kerwin, K. "Metamemory and Motivation: A Comparison of Strategy Use and Performance in German and American Children." *Journal of Cross-Cultural Psychology,* 1986, *17,* 315–336.

Schraw, G., Bruning, R., and Svoboda, C. "The Effect of Reader Purpose on Interest and Recall." *Journal of Reading Behavior,* 1995, *27,* 1–17.

Schraw, G., and Lehman, S. "Situational Interest: A Review of the Literature and Directions for Future Research." *Educational Psychology Review,* 2001, *13,* 23–52.

Seifert, T. L., and O'Keefe, B. A. "The Relationship of Work Avoidance and Learning Goals to Perceived Competence, Externality and Meaning." *British Journal of Educational Psychology,* 2001, *71,* 81–92.

Seligman, M.E.P. *The Optimistic Child.* New York: HarperCollins, 1995.

Shen, C., and Pedulla, J. J. "The Relationship Between Students' Achievement and Their Self-Perception of Competence and Rigour of Mathematics and Science: A Cross-National Analysis." *Assessment in Education,* 2000, *7,* 237–253.

Steinberg, L. *Beyond the Classroom: Why School Reform Has Failed and What Parents Need to Do.* New York: Touchstone Books, 1996.

Stevenson, H. W., Chen, C., and Uttal, D. H. "Beliefs and Achievement: A Study of Black, Anglo and Hispanic Children." *Child Development,* 1990, *61,* 508–523.

Stevenson, H. W., Lee, S., and Stigler, J. W. "Mathematics Achievement of Chinese, Japanese, and American Children." *Science,* 1986, *231,* 693–699.

Stevenson, H. W., and Nerison-Low, R. *To Sum It Up: Case Studies of Education in Germany, Japan, and the United States.* Washington, D.C.: National Institute on Student Achievement, Curriculum and Assessment, U.S. Department of Education, 1998.

Stevenson, H. W., and Stigler, J. W. *The Learning Gap: Why Our Schools Are Failing and What We Can Learn from Japanese and Chinese Education.* New York: Simon & Schuster, 1992.

Sykes, C. J. *Dumbing Down Our Kids.* New York: St. Martin's Press, 1995.

Vrugt, A. "Perceived Self-Efficacy, Social Comparison, Affective Reactions and Academic Performance." *British Journal of Educational Psychology,* 1994, *64,* 465–472.

Wade, S., Buxton, W. M., and Kelly, M. "Using Think-Alouds to Examine Reader-Text Interest." *Reading Research Quarterly,* 1999, *34,* 194–216.

Weiner, B. "A Theory of Motivation for Some Classroom Experiences." *Journal of Educational Psychology,* 1979, *71,* 3–25.

Wheldall, K., and Merrett, F. *The Behavioural Approach to Teaching Package (BAT-PACK).* Birmingham, England: Positive Products, 1985.

White, M. A. "Natural Rates of Teacher Approval and Disapproval in the Classroom." *Journal of Applied Behavior Analysis,* 1975, *8,* 367–372.

Wolters, C. A. "Self-Regulated Learning and College Students' Regulation of Motivation." *Journal of Educational Psychology,* 1998, *90,* 224–235.

Wyatt, W. J., and Hawkins, R. P. "Rates of Teachers' Verbal Approval and Disapproval." *Behavior Modification,* 1987, *11,* 27–51.

Wylie, R. *The Self-Concept.* Lincoln: University of Nebraska Press, 1979.

Yair, G. "Reforming Motivation: How the Structure of Instruction Affects Students' Learning Experiences." *British Educational Research Journal,* 2000, *26,* 191–210.

Ziomek, R., and Svec, J. "High School Grades and Activity: Evidence of Grade Inflation." *NASSP Bulletin,* 1997, *81,* 105–113.

NEIL HUFTON is principal lecturer in education at the School of Education, University of Sunderland, England.

JULIAN G. ELLIOTT is professor of educational psychology and associate dean at the School of Education, University of Sunderland, England.

LEONID ILLUSHIN is senior lecturer in education at Hertzen State University, St. Petersburg, Russia.

5

Research on beliefs about intelligence used questionnaires to characterize students as viewing intelligence as either a malleable quality or a fixed trait. In our study, regardless of the belief they endorsed, all students spoke about intelligence as malleable in subsequent interviews.

Implicit Theories of Intelligence Across Academic Domains: A Study of Meaning Making in Adolescents of Mexican Descent

Gisell Quihuis, Janine Bempechat, Norma V. Jimenez, Beth A. Boulay

Research on implicit theories of intelligence has highlighted the degree to which children's beliefs about ability influence task choices and persistence in novel achievement situations (Bempechat, London, and Dweck, 1991; Dweck and Bempechat, 1983; Dweck, Chiu, and Hong, 1995). Specifically, children who believe that intelligence is malleable and unlimited (incremental theorists) tend to prefer challenging over nonchallenging tasks, even when their confidence is low. When faced with difficulty or failure, incremental theorists tend to display mastery-oriented behavior. In other words, they become persistent and engage in effective problem-solving strategies, such as self-monitoring. Given their orientation toward increasing skills and knowledge, issues of ability, in the normative sense, are not salient for incremental theorists.

In contrast, children who believe that intelligence is both limited and limiting (entity theorists) tend to avoid challenge when their confidence is low and opt for tasks that ensure success. When faced with difficulty or failure, entity theorists tend to succumb to learned helplessness. That is, they have been shown to give up relatively quickly and display ineffective problem-solving strategies, such as perseveration. According to the theory, issues of competence are rather salient for them; by definition, they have reason to doubt or question their intelligence. However, when their confidence is high, they tend to resemble incremental theorists in their achievement behaviors. That is, they opt for challenging tasks and display mastery-oriented behavior in the face of difficulty.

This work has been invaluable in helping educators understand children's differential approaches to learning. However, fundamental methodological and conceptual problems limit the degree to which we can both generalize and apply these findings in school settings (Schunk, 1995; Weiner, 1995). The identification of entity and incremental theorists has occurred exclusively in the context of experimental studies, in which forced-choice or Likert-style questions are used to classify students into one of the two categories of implicit beliefs (Dweck and Henderson, 1989). We have recently argued that this method of inquiry reduces students' beliefs to dichotomies, resulting in characterizations that are unrealistic and fail to address the contexts in which students' learning takes place (Bempechat and Boulay, 2001).

As several researchers have noted, it is quite conceivable that individuals may hold aspects of both theories simultaneously, depending on situational factors (that is, teacher feedback; see Lewis, 1995; Nicholls, 1983; Schunk, 1995). For example, Anderson (1995) has argued that the fact that the theories can be so easily manipulated suggests that individuals can simultaneously hold the knowledge structures inherent in both entity and incremental theories, but choose to make use of one or the other structure in a given situation.

Furthermore, this methodological approach has created a condition in which the research has imposed abstract categories on students' understandings. We know very little about students' emic concepts of intelligence—those idiosyncratic and contextualized perspectives bound by parameters defined by the students themselves. Indeed, while documenting the varieties of intelligence, Gardner (1983) argued that the exclusive use of surveys to assess children's notions of their own intelligence deprives us of the opportunity to capitalize on what they perceive as their own intellectual strengths and weaknesses. In this regard, it is very interesting that Nicholls (1990) believes that it is not particularly helpful for researchers to focus on how students perceive or conceptualize ability. According to Nicholls, researchers should focus their efforts on exploring the meanings that students attach to their work (see also Holloway, 1988). Rather than asking how children judge ability, Nicholls argues that much richer information can be gleaned from asking children what they think ability is—its underlying meanings—and how these differ as a function of student characteristics, such as age, ethnicity, and social class. In direct support of emic research, he cautions that we need to be careful not to project our own conceptions of ability onto children. Thus, it is important to probe the degree to which students' classification as entity or incremental theorists is consistent with their expressed views and understandings.

In addition, Dweck and her colleagues have focused on conceptions of ability across domains of the self, such as intellectual, social, and physical skills and physical appearance (Bempechat, London, and Dweck, 1991), and have not examined the degree to which children may adhere to different theories in different academic domains. Clearly, for example, some students may lean toward an entity theory in mathematics but hold an incremental theory in language arts.

The fact that the literature has relied exclusively on white middle-class children presents a conceptual problem. We find ourselves in a time when our school-aged population is becoming increasingly diverse, and educators are most concerned about the performance of poor and minority students. Sensitivity to the ways in which ethnic minority parents understand intelligence may help teachers support their students' learning and achievement. For example, among Latino families, including those of Mexican descent, being educated carries both intellectual and moral meanings. The purpose of formal schooling is not simply to highlight unequal abilities and mastery of content material, but to socialize children toward morality and appropriate social behavior that would have a positive influence on their character.

Thus, a high-achieving student who does not treat her parents *con respeto* (respectfully), is not *acomedida* (helpful without being asked), or does not conform to role expectations in the household is not considered *bien educada* (well educated) (Reese, Balzano, Gallimore, and Goldenberg, 1995; Valdés, 1996). For girls in particular, family and household obligations are as important as, and sometimes more important than, scholastic ones. Valdés (1996) reports that parents living in the United States will take their children to Mexico during the school year if the entire family is needed to fulfill an obligation, such as attending a funeral.

Furthermore, as Gallimore and his colleagues have reported, concerns over moral development are such that parents may forgo a unique educational opportunity for a child. Their ethnographic study described a case in which a teenage girl was recommended by her mathematics teacher for an advanced mathematics course at another school, an event that would be considered an honor for many parents. Instead, these parents did not allow her to attend, citing concerns over negative influences to which she might be exposed at this other school.

The purpose of this study, then, was to address these gaps in the literature. Given our primary interest in how students speak about their conceptions of ability, we focused on adolescents, who relative to elementary school students have greater cognitive capacity for insight and reflection. We combined the traditional quantitative approach to assessing theories of intelligence with qualitative interviews, thus allowing us the opportunity to discern how students speak of and understand their implicit beliefs about ability across four academic domains (general ability, mathematics, science, and English). As a first step in addressing these issues in ethnic minority students, we surveyed and interviewed a group of low-income adolescents of Mexican descent.

Method

Fifty-seven English-proficient, low-income, first-generation Mexican American tenth through twelfth graders participated in this study (thirty-five females, twenty-two males). The average annual income of the participating families was $15,435. In all, thirteen of these students took part in a follow-up interview session. The students were enrolled in a public high school in southern California. All participating students were bilingual in English and Spanish. They were recruited through announcements made in class. Permission to participate was granted by both parents and students themselves through permission slips sent home from school. The response rate was approximately 80 percent.

Instruments

We used the traditional questionnaire method to assess students' beliefs about their abilities. We then went one step further by interviewing a subset of students about the beliefs that they endorsed.

Theories of Intelligence Questionnaire. Following Dweck and Henderson (1989), adherence to entity and incremental beliefs was assessed through two six-point Likert-type questions in each of the four domains: general intelligence, mathematics, science, and English. Each question was posed as an entity statement, to which students indicated their degree of agreement. Students responded to these eight questions in approximately ten minutes.

Again, following Dweck and Henderson (1989), for each domain, students' responses to the two theory questions were added, yielding a scoring range from 2 to 12. An a priori decision was made to classify as incremental theorists those students who showed any level of disagreement with the entity statement. Thus, students who scored anywhere from 2 to 6 were classified as entity theorists in the particular domain. Students who scored anywhere from 7 to 12 were classified as incremental theorists in the particular domain.

Follow-Up Interview. A semistructured interview guide was developed to probe students' theory choice in each domain. Specifically, we presented students with their previously completed questionnaires and asked that they elaborate on their responses. The interview lasted approximately one hour.

Procedure

A volunteer teacher with no knowledge of the work on theories of intelligence administered the questionnaire to participating students in a group setting. He read from an instruction sheet that had been provided by the first author. Based on their theory classifications, thirteen students (six female, seven male) were selected for one-hour individual interviews, which took place approximately one month later.

Results

Students were classified as Entity or Incremental theorists according to the procedure outlined by Dweck and Henderson (1989). A cross section of students endorsing different theories were then interviewed.

Questionnaire Classifications. In classifying students across the domains, three combinations of beliefs were possible: entity theorist in all domains (which we labeled Entity-All), incremental theorist in all domains (Incremental-All), and some combination of entity and incremental theorist in different domains (Mixed). This classification procedure yielded four Entity-All (one female, three males), thirty-seven Incremental-All (twenty-six females, eleven males), and sixteen Mixed theorists (eight females, eight males). The theory classifications as a function of domain are presented in Table 5.1.

Interviews. Thirteen students were selected for interviews on the basis of their theory classification: the four Entity-All students, the three Incremental-All students with the highest incremental scores in each domain, and six Mixed students who represented different combinations of theories across the domains. There was no domain-specific pattern of theory preference among these students (see Table 5.2). For example, only one of the six students declared an entity theory in both quantitative domains (such as mathematics and science).

Incremental-All. Interviews revealed that the Incremental-All students expressed beliefs that unequivocally reflected a malleable view of ability in

Table 5.1. Number of Entity and Incremental Theorists Across Academic Domains

| | | General Intelligence—Entity | | General Intelligence—Incremental | |
		Math Entity	Math Incremental	Math Entity	Math Incremental
Science Entity	English Entity	4	5	1	0
	English Incremental	0	1	0	2
Science Incremental	English Entity	2	0	0	0
	English Incremental	2	1	2	37

Table 5.2. Theory Classifications of Mixed Theorists

Student	Domain			
	General Intelligence	Math	Science	English
1 (female)	E	I	E	E
2 (female)	E	I	E	E
3 (female)	E	I	E	E
4 (male)	I	E	E	I
5 (female)	I	E	I	I
6 (male)	E	E	I	E

Note: E = entity; I = incremental.

each domain. For example, Ruben, a sophomore, believed that effort and desire make a crucial difference in learning. He saw no limits to intelligence and felt it is not a fixed quality. He attributed failure in learning to a lack of effort and interest or to negative experiences, but not to a lack of intelligence. He believed intelligence is a developmental quality that increases with learning:

> I don't think there is a limit. I think the person, if he really motivates himself and wants to learn, he can learn many things because there have been things that I have said that I thought I would not be able to learn, but I did. So the lazy person who does not want to or does not put effort into it, then there the person places a limit on himself. But the person who wants to do it puts effort into it. There is no limit in intelligence. Intelligence involves all subjects, and if there is no limit in intelligence, then there is no limit in the rest of the subjects.

Ruben acknowledged that although some things may be difficult to learn initially, a person can learn provided that he or she puts forth enough effort. He also believed that the difference between those who achieve academically and those who do not lies in the desire to do so and the willingness to invest effort in a task.

Pablo attributed any failure or any limits in learning to a bad instructor or a lack of attention on the student's behalf. He also raised the issue of ease in learning by expressing the belief that regardless of the subject area, students learn at varying levels, independent of their actual intelligence, as illustrated in the following exchange:

PABLO: I think that everyone can learn if he wants, except that there are some that take longer to learn and that's all. It's like everything. One can learn anything just wanting to.

INTERVIEWER: Okay. What about those that take longer to learn? Why is that so?

PABLO: I couldn't say. I think that . . . I guess they understand things slower.

INTERVIEWER: So do you think that that person is less intelligent or the same, just slower?

PABLO: They are equally intelligent; it's just that they take longer to think about things.

Entity-All. Four students, according to the questionnaire, adhered to entity beliefs across all four intellectual areas. In their interviews, all began by describing the degree to which they believed in the immutability of intelligence. With some elaboration, however, this view gave way to beliefs that were wholly consistent with incremental views. The students attributed any limits in learning to factors other than mental capacity, including loss of motivation, effort, or desire to learn; laziness; previous negative educational experiences; and incompetent teachers.

For example, Rubi, a junior, offered what appears to be a classic definition of an entity view of intelligence—a quality that is both limited and limiting—as follows: "I think that intelligence, you have to be born with it. It's something that, that . . . I don't know. How can I explain it? I don't believe it's something that you learn through your environment, you know? You can't develop it. You are actually born with it." However, Rubi later acknowledged that intelligence is a quality that grows, as illustrated by the following exchange about geometry, a course in which she was experiencing difficulty:

RUBI: I tried. I liked geometry and then the teacher I had, I went after school but I did not learn, and that's why I think I did not like geometry 'cuz I did not understand it.

INTERVIEWER: Knowing that, do you think there is a limit to how much math you could learn? Do you think you could go on to more advanced levels of math and understand them?

RUBI: Yes, I think I could.

INTERVIEWER: How would you go about accomplishing that?

RUBI: I would, depends on the teacher, get tutoring.

INTERVIEWER: That would make the difference and allow you to go on?

RUBI: Yes. Just like in science—if I really needed it to go off to college or needed it for my career, I would break my head for it.

Julian, a junior, adhered to different views of intelligence, depending on the subject, as demonstrated by the following discussion:

JULIAN: I feel that I know something and that I have a certain amount of intelligence, but that I can't change it—can't make it better or use it. Some subjects you can, and others you can't. In math, sometimes yes, but biology is not the same. I don't think I could change it. Maybe if I tried, but I have not tried.

INTERVIEWER: What's the difference between math and biology? Why can you change it in math and not in biology?

JULIAN: Biology has strange words, and they all seem similar at times, and not so in math.

INTERVIEWER: Isn't that just related to the language?

JULIAN: Maybe, how you pronounce them, but I don't really think so.

INTERVIEWER: Why do you think that you can't change your intelligence in any subject?

JULIAN: Due to the subject; it depends on the subject.

Julian also noted that individual effort plays an important role in intelligence. Specifically, he argued that while laziness would prevent an individual from acquiring new knowledge, any limits on learning would stem from the individual's intelligence:

INTERVIEWER: Here [on the questionnaire] you said there was a limit to intelligence.

JULIAN: It also depends on the person. If he's lazy and doesn't want to learn, then there will be a limit right off.

INTERVIEWER: Then the limit has to do with what—the intelligence or the motivation of the person? Where is the limit?

JULIAN: With the intelligence.

INTERVIEWER: What if the person is very motivated and tries and tries?

JULIAN: He can do it too.

INTERVIEWER: What about intelligence?

JULIAN: If there is none, I don't think he'll make it.

INTERVIEWER: Is intelligence something one is born with that can't be changed?

JULIAN: Yes.

INTERVIEWER: If you are born with a certain amount of intelligence and study a lot, will you become more intelligent?

JULIAN: If you are intelligent, you see things, and you know them more or less. I don't think that you can do more. There, with the intelligence you have . . . you were born with . . . with that you do it, learn.

Mixed Theorists. Each Mixed theorist endorsed a different theory in different domains. Results showed that students who endorsed an incremental theory were unwavering in their beliefs that intelligence is a malleable quality. Again, those who endorsed an entity theory initially spoke of intelligence in fixed terms, but soon elaborated views that very much reflected notions of intelligence as a flexible quality. For example, Isabel, a tenth grader, endorsed an entity theory in general intelligence but an incremental theory in English, mathematics, and science. She articulated the following about general intelligence:

ISABEL: Intelligence is not fixed because if I have the will, I think I can become more intelligent.

INTERVIEWER: Can you explain your answer to this question about intelligence?

ISABEL: Well, I don't know. Well, if I have a certain amount of intelligence, it only reaches so far, and that's it. I can't do anything about it.

INTERVIEWER: Do you think you can increase your intelligence?

ISABEL: Yes. I think intelligence can grow. I think so. Well, yes, because I would keep learning every day more, and my intelligence would increase because I have learned new things. That's why intelligence would get bigger.

Discontinuities Between Questionnaires and Interviews

The most interesting finding of this research is that across the domains, students who were designated as entity theorists (Entity-All and Entity within Mixed) spoke initially of their beliefs with the characteristic uncertainty and low confidence associated with fixed views. Yet when asked to elaborate on their beliefs, they asserted positions that were consistent with incremental theory and articulated the kinds of mastery-oriented strategies ordinarily associated with incremental beliefs. In a direct challenge to Dweck's theory, we propose that when confidence is low, entity theorists are able to articulate effective strategies for achieving success, particularly when the need to perform well is high (for example, successfully completing a college entrance requirement).

Using a different methodology allowed us to demonstrate that the same individual can hold different theories in the same domain, as Lewis (1995) speculated. It is possible that our qualitative methodology revealed what Darley (1995) refers to as the "optimistic entity theorist" (p. 291). That is, despite what may be a record of relatively poor performance, these students believe that they have the ability to succeed in a domain in which they have experienced difficulty. These students could be simultaneously holding aspects of the knowledge structures inherent in both theories, as elaborated by Anderson (1995; see also Schunk, 1995). This suggests that entity theorists with low confidence may indeed be capable of demonstrating mastery-oriented strategies in the face of challenge, much like their incremental counterparts. Because we did not study behavior, this notion is speculative, and we plan to address it directly in our next research project.

How can we reconcile the interpretation of our findings with Dweck's theory? Our view is that for entity theorists, achievement beliefs expressed in a decontextualized experimental setting are likely to vary considerably from those asserted in an interview designed to elicit the meanings students attach to their beliefs. Responding to interview questions allowed these students to place their beliefs in the context of day-to-day learning in which a variety of social (such as teacher expectancies and peer influence), structural (such as tracking), and internal (such as the value placed on a given subject) factors are likely to play a role in their achievement views.

Those classified as incremental theorists expressed beliefs altogether consistent with their designated theory. Why did we observe this consistency only for incremental theorists? Recall that by definition, incremental theorists are oriented toward expanding their skills and knowledge, regardless of confidence level. Thus, relative to entity theorists, incremental theorists do not need to question their intelligence to the same extent. To do so would be self-defeating, in that these students would be implicitly acknowledging that there may be limits to their intelligence. For similar reasons, we would expect entity theorists with high confidence to articulate strategies for achieving success in the face of difficulty.

Recall our interest in measuring students' beliefs across academic domains. While Dweck has previously reported a tendency to find the majority of students in a given sample to be incremental theorists in terms of their general beliefs about ability (Dweck, Chiu, and Hong, 1995), we found this tendency to hold true across academic domains. Among the students who held different beliefs in different academic domains, it is interesting that we found no systemic pattern of beliefs, nor did we find systematic gender differences. (It is important to keep in mind that our sample of Mixed theorists was relatively small: sixteen students. Perhaps systematic patterns may emerge in a larger sample of students who hold different theories in academic domains.) That is, we did not find that students who were entity theorists in mathematics were also entity theorists in science, a related domain. This could be due to differential classroom experiences throughout their schooling in general, and their present school experiences in particular. In other words, it could be that given the ways in which classroom variables differ (teacher beliefs and competitive versus cooperative classrooms, for example), it is conceivable that a student who is very unsure of her ability in mathematics could be very optimistic about her potential in science, given, for example, a classroom setting that minimizes social comparison (see Nicholls, 1989).

This study reports the first findings on theories of intelligence in American ethnic minority students. Clearly, students' beliefs about learning do not develop in a vacuum. They are very much influenced by the achievement beliefs of their parents, peers, and teachers, as well as the social, cultural, and academic environments in which they are growing (Ames and Archer, 1987; Bempechat, Graham, and Jimenez, 1999; Ogbu, 1986; Peak, 1991). It is in this context that researchers within cultural psychology and cognitive anthropology agree that the psychological study of individuals must be situated within their culture and that culture itself serves to guide psychosocial development (Bruner, 1996; Haste, 1994; LeVine, 1977). We cannot continue to think about traditional theories of psychology and development as universal (Markus, Mullally, and Kitayama, 1997); all human development takes place within a particular time, context, and culture (Roopnarine and Carter, 1992; Sinha and Sinha, 1997). A context-free, culture-free environment simply does not exist (Bronfenbrenner, 1979; LeVine, Miller, and West, 1988; Shweder, 1990).

It is, of course, inappropriate to generalize our findings to other Latino subgroups. More systematic research is needed across other ethnic and social class groups. For example, given the increased concerns about the underachievement of ethnic minorities in urban settings, it would be very interesting to know how high- and low-achieving African American teenagers speak about and understand their theories of intelligence.

Furthermore, it is clear to us that the rich, varied, and complex beliefs that exist along the continuum between entity and incremental theories have been largely untapped. Can an incremental theorist be concerned about grades? Of course. Can an entity theorist entertain the notion and take the risk of learning a new and challenging task? Most certainly. We assert that in order to attain a deeper understanding of how children's achievement behavior is influenced by their implicit beliefs about ability, we must integrate achievement motivation theory, with its focus on achievement-related cognitions, with principles that have emerged in cultural psychology. It is critical that we recognize that cognitive processes and factors in the cultural and social environment are not independent; one cannot separate the individual from the context (Bronfenbrenner, 1979; Haste, 1994; Vygotsky, 1978). Therefore, it is important that future research incorporate both individual meaning making and an appreciation of the social and cultural contexts in which students learn. In other words, how do students speak about and understand their learning experiences? What are the rich and varied ways in which they make meaning of peer, family, and teacher influences that both foster and hinder their academic achievement?

Indeed, the issue is much larger than a simple two-dimensional classification of students' achievement beliefs. As we have demonstrated in this study, students' achievement beliefs are anything but two-dimensional; they are rich and complex. If our goal is to help teachers meet the educational needs of their students, we must provide them with information that is authentic and meaningful to them. This means that we need to understand, from the students' perspectives, the ways in which they interpret difficulty or failure, the dimensions they choose to use when describing themselves as learners, and the classroom experiences they perceive to help or hinder their academic progress. Importantly, we need to acknowledge that these will differ for different students. In all likelihood, however, similar themes will emerge over the course of interviews with many students. For example, our qualitative, longitudinal study of urban, Catholic high school students is revealing that their experiences of support and caring from faculty motivate them to want to excel in school (Bempechat and others, 2001).

We are not advocating that traditional quantitative methods of inquiry, such as Likert-type scales and surveys, be abandoned. Rather, we believe that research that uses mixed and multiple methods to understand students' theories of intelligence will yield a richer understanding of the influence of students' achievement beliefs on their achievement behaviors. As we have recently argued, the results of questionnaires can inform qualitative interviews, which can help refine the design of further quantitative inquiry (Bempechat, Jimenez, and Boulay, forthcoming).

Conclusion

This research illustrates the centrality of examining meaning making in context and points to the critical role that qualitative methodology plays. By focusing on students' emic concepts of intelligence, we have extended our knowledge of the ways they understand their achievement beliefs and experiences and the ways in which these understandings may influence their approaches to learning. Future research should examine the degree to which students' articulated beliefs and strategies for coping with academic uncertainty are realized in their classroom behavior. In addition, we must make a concerted effort to examine understandings of ability concepts across a diverse group of students.

References

Ames, C., and Archer, J. "Mothers' Beliefs About the Role of Ability and Effort in School Learning." *Journal of Educational Psychology,* 1987, 71, 409–414.

Anderson, C. "Implicit Theories in Broad Perspective." *Psychological Inquiry,* 1995, 6, 286–290.

Bempechat, J., and Boulay, B. A. "Beyond Dichotomous Characterizations: New Directions in Achievement Motivation Research." In D. McInerney and S. Van Etten (eds.), *Research on Sociocultural Influences on Motivation and Learning.* Greenwich, Conn.: Information Age Publishing, 2001.

Bempechat, J., Graham, S., and Jimenez, N. V. "The Socialization of Achievement in Poor and Minority Students: A Comparative Study." *Journal of Cross-Cultural Psychology,* 1999, *30,* 139–158.

Bempechat, J., Jimenez, N. V., and Boulay, B. A. *The Cultural Contexts of Schooling: Implications for the Design, Conduct, and Analysis of International Studies.* Washington, D.C.: National Academy of Science/National Research Council, forthcoming.

Bempechat, J., London, P., and Dweck, C. "Children's Conceptions of Ability in Major Domains: An Interview and Experimental Study." *Child Study Journal,* 1991, *21,* 11–36.

Bempechat, J., and others. *Achievement and Motivation in Catholic High School Students: A Qualitative Study.* Unpublished manuscript, Harvard University, 2001.

Bronfenbrenner, U. *The Ecology of Human Development.* Cambridge, Mass.: Harvard University Press, 1979.

Bruner, J. *The Culture of Education.* Cambridge, Mass.: Harvard University Press, 1996.

Darley, J. "Mutable Theories That Organize the World." *Psychological Inquiry,* 1995, *6,* 290–293.

Dweck, C., and Bempechat, J. "Children's Theories of Intelligence: Consequences for Learning." In S. Paris, G. Olsen, and H. Stevenson (eds.), *Learning and Motivation in the Classroom.* Mahwah, N.J.: Erlbaum, 1983.

Dweck, C., Chiu, C., and Hong, Y. "Implicit Theories and Their Role in Judgments and Reactions: A World from Two Perspectives." *Psychological Inquiry,* 1995, *6,* 267–285.

Dweck, C., and Henderson, V. "Theories of Intelligence: Background and Measures." Paper presented at the biennial meetings of the Society for Research in Child Development, Kansas City, Apr. 1989.

Gardner, H. "The Development of Competence in Culturally Defined Domains: A Preliminary Framework." In R. Shweder and R. A. LeVine (eds.), *Culture Theory: Essays on Mind, Self, and Emotion.* Cambridge, England: Cambridge University Press, 1983.

Haste, H. *The Sexual Metaphor.* Cambridge, Mass.: Harvard University Press, 1994.

Holloway, S. D. "Concepts of Ability and Effort in Japan and the United States." *Review of Educational Research,* 1988, *58,* 327–345.

LeVine, R. A. "Child Rearing as Cultural Adaptation." In P. Leiderman, S. Tulkin, and A. Rosenfeld (eds.), *Culture and Infancy: Variations in the Human Experience.* Orlando, Fla.: Academic Press, 1977.

LeVine, R. A., Miller, P. M., and West, M. M. (eds.). *Parental Behavior in Diverse Societies.* New Directions for Child Development, no. 40. San Francisco: Jossey-Bass, 1988.

Lewis, M. "The Nature of Cause, the Role of Antecedent Conditions in Children's Attribution, and Emotional Behavior." *Psychological Inquiry,* 1995, *6,* 305–307.

Markus, H. R., Mullally, P. R., and Kitayama, S. "Selfways: Diversity in Modes of Cultural Participation." In U. Neisser and D. A. Jopling (eds.), *The Conceptual Self in Context: Culture, Experience, Self-Understanding.* Cambridge, England: Cambridge University Press, 1997.

Nicholls, J. G. "Conceptions of Ability and Achievement Motivation: A Theory and Its Implications for Education." In S. Paris, G. Olsen, and H. Stevenson (eds.), *Learning and Motivation in the Classroom.* Mahwah, N.J.: Erlbaum, 1983.

Nicholls, J. G. *The Competitive Ethos and Democratic Education.* Cambridge, Mass.: Harvard University Press, 1989.

Nicholls, J. G. "What Is Ability and Why Are We Mindful of It? A Developmental Perspective." In R. Sternberg and J. Kolligian (eds.), *Competence Considered.* New Haven, Conn.: Yale University Press, 1990.

Ogbu, J. "The Consequences of the American Caste System." In U. Neisser (ed.), *The School Achievement of Minority Children: New Perspectives*. Mahwah, N.J.: Erlbaum, 1986.

Peak, L. *Learning to Go to School in Japan*. Berkeley: University of California Press, 1991.

Reese, L., Balzano, S., Gallimore, R., and Goldenberg, C. "The Concept of 'Educaciòn': Latino Family Values and American Schooling." *International Journal of Education Research*, 1995, *23*, 57–81.

Roopnarine, J., and Carter, D. B. "The Cultural Context of Socialization: A Much Ignored Issue!" In J. Roopnarine and D. B. Carter (eds.), *Annual Advances in Applied Developmental Psychology*, Vol. 5: *Parent-Child Socialization in Diverse Cultures*. Norwood, N.J.: Ablex, 1992.

Schunk, D. "Implicit Theories and Achievement Behavior." *Psychological Inquiry*, 1995, *6*, 311–314.

Shweder, R. "Cultural Psychology—What Is It?" In J. Stigler, R. Shweder, and G. Herdt (eds.), *Cultural Psychology: Essays on Comparative Human Development*. Cambridge, England: Cambridge University Press, 1990.

Sinha, D., and Sinha, M. "Orientations to Psychology: Asian and Western." In H. Kao and D. Sinha (eds.), *Asian Perspectives on Psychology*. Vol. 19. Thousand Oaks, Calif.: Sage, 1997.

Valdés, G. *Con Respeto: Bridging the Distances Between Culturally Diverse Families and Schools*. New York: Teachers College Press, 1996.

Vygotsky, L. *Mind in Society*. (M. Cole, V. John-Steiner, S. Scribner, and E. Souberman, eds.). Cambridge, Mass.: Harvard University Press, 1978.

Weiner, B. "Lessons from the Past." *Psychological Inquiry*, 1995, *6*, 319–321.

GISELL QUIHUIS is director of outcomes and evaluation at EMQ Children and Family Services, Campbell, California.

JANINE BEMPECHAT is senior consultant at the Program for Educational Change Agents, Eliot-Pearson Department of Child Development, Tufts University, Medford, Massachusetts.

NORMA V. JIMENEZ is instructor in education at the Harvard Graduate School of Education.

BETH A. BOULAY is an advanced doctoral student at the Harvard Graduate School of Education.

6

*Previous chapters in this volume outline a new
methodology of achievement motivation, an approach
that seeks to identify the cultural and personal meanings
of educational performance through methods that clarify
its multiple contexts.*

Contexts and Culture in Psychological Research

Robert A. LeVine

Psychologists have a credibility problem that is on exhibit in this volume.
Some people believe that psychological research instruments (tests, interviews, and questionnaires, for example) measure what they are intended to
measure (abilities, attitudes, motives, personality traits), but many others
do not. And some social scientists cast doubt on any psychological explanations for individual behavior, favoring explanations in terms of environmental variables (incentives, normative models, situational constraints, or
opportunity structures) rather than personal dispositions. But even those
inclined to accept the plausibility of psychological explanation in general
often challenge the validity of specific assessment methods. This is true of
research on educational achievement, with major implications for policy
and practice.

Within the discipline of psychology, the credibility problem has been
treated as a methodological crisis. For much of the past half-century, concerns about the ecological validity of psychological experiments, the conver-
gent validity of personality tests, and artifacts in attitude research have been
raised in social, personality, and developmental psychology, sending personality psychology into decline and investigators of child development into
naturalistic observations and changing the way research is justified in academic journals. A central question has been the extent to which psychological methods capture responses genuinely symptomatic of the underlying
dispositions they are designed to assess or only superficial reactions to the
conditions of measurement.

In social psychology, this issue produced the artifact crisis of the
1960s, in which it was argued that responses to scales constructed to assess

particular attitudes are confounded with generalized response sets such as acquiescence and social desirability bias and that the findings of experimental studies are influenced by investigator expectations and the situation-specific reactions of human subjects. In psychometric research, issues of test-taking ability and familiarity effects have posed similar challenges to psychological investigators, while interview studies are plagued by an awareness that interviewer bias and the differential verbal fluency of respondents can affect their results. Psychologists have proved adept at adjusting methodological standards to counter these artifacts and biases but have been far from successful in dispelling doubts about their conventional methods of collecting data. There has been a rising tide of skepticism of those methods among the overlapping research communities that consume as well as produce psychological research findings and an increasing sense, even among psychologists themselves, that more needs to be done to supplement formal methods with contextual and even ethnographic research (Jessor, Colby, and Shweder, 1996).

This volume represents the quest to break out of the mold into which psychologists put themselves during the first decades of the twentieth century when they embraced experiments and psychometrics as the only methods for scientific research. Its chapters show that if psychological research is to answer questions raised by cross-national studies of educational performance, it must go beyond the conventional procedures of formal assessment. The editors begin by highlighting three problems: the limitations of survey research conducted without contextual investigation, the understanding of key concepts in diverse cultural contexts, and the description and explanation of individual differences within culturally distinct groups being compared. In Chapter One, they review the most relevant literature and point out the pitfalls—speculation, oversimplification, contradictions—in interpreting the results of cross-national studies such as the Third International Mathematics and Science Study (TIMSS) without detailed contextual evidence. Failure to include historical and cultural evidence leaves investigators guessing at meanings that could be studied empirically, though not through the standard measures of quantitative assessment. They illustrate, convincingly in my opinion, the richness and complexity of students' views concerning their own school performance, and they invite us to see this richness and complexity not as disorderly and confusing but as a pathway to the kind of valid understanding that can assist educational policy-making.

Bempechat and Elliott's call for more authentic forms of inquiry on achievement motivation, that is, for a broader range of research methods and greater concern about the convergence of evidence collected from different sources, opens the door to informative explorations of the psychological factors lying behind student performance. As a counter to the tendency to reify polarities emerging from one set of studies (effort versus ability, entity versus incremental) as though they represented the actual dispositions of national populations, they recommend a closer and fuller examination of cultural differences, indigenous concepts, historical contexts, and subnational variations. They mention the paradox that instructional methods often criticized as ineffective in the Western countries that generated them are considered liberating innovations when imported into China and other non-Western countries. This suggests an important line of investigation into the way pedagogical traditions create social contexts that can have differential effects on learning. Bempechat and Elliott also propose that researchers pay attention to the opportunity structures facing students and their parents in different countries and socioeconomic settings, as environmental factors that influence motivation as much as students' beliefs and attributions.

TIMSS provides a culture-specific example of the larger context to which Bempechat and Elliott are calling attention. The average performance of Japanese eighth-grade students ranked very high on mathematics compared to other countries, and Stigler's videotaped study of eighth-grade math teachers in Japan, Germany, and the United States showed that the Japanese teachers taught mathematics concepts far more than their counterparts in the other two countries did (Stigler and Hiebert, 1999). One could conclude on this basis that the learning of conceptual mathematics accounted for the superior performance of the Japanese students. But it is also true that a majority of the Japanese students who took the eighth-grade TIMSS were attending *juku,* that is, private tutoring schools that drill them in mathematics, among other things. Perhaps this drilling is what really counts. Or perhaps the parents of students attending *juku,* having paid for out-of-school tutoring, press the students to perform well. Or perhaps the students whose parents have paid for tutoring feel obliged to work harder to meet their parents' expectations. All of these are plausible hypotheses; only direct interviewing and observations can evaluate which of them is empirically sound and which is not. The more data that are considered, the less the investigators' conclusions are the captives of a particular method and the more valid they are likely to be.

Chapters Two through Five provide cases illustrating both the puzzles emerging from cross-national research and the promise of qualitative data in resolving them. Holloway and Behrens begin in Chapter Two with the apparent paradox emerging from previous studies that Japanese mothers express less confidence in their parenting abilities than mothers from other industrial countries, though outside observers tend to describe Japanese mothering in positive terms and Japanese child rearing as indulgent. In their own study of forty mothers in Sapporo, however, the subjects rated their efficacy as parents highly on a questionnaire used in different countries and described their own experience as children in negative terms in open-ended interviews. Holloway and Behrens explain that the open-ended interviews preceding the questionnaire may have led the mothers to relax and set aside the culturally appropriate modesty that had deflated parenting efficacy scores in previous studies, resulting in substantially higher scores. Although they do not invoke ethnographic evidence, there are abundant data that support this interpretation of the efficacy results.

Japanese adult behavior has long been described by anthropologists as reflecting a role perfectionism that involves heightened awareness of public standards of role performance and, as a consequence, self-criticism and underestimating one's performance in public situations, which can appear automatically as extreme modesty when a Japanese man or woman is questioned about how well he or she does in a particular role (DeVos, 1972; Lebra, 1976). An approach that facilitates informality and intimacy in the research relationship seems to be needed to overcome the reflex of modesty that questionnaires can elicit in a Japanese context and reach the private assessments adults are making of their performance. Holloway and Behrens provided this approach in their open-ended interviews.

Their approach seems also to have facilitated in the mothers disclosures that their own mothers were strict and "scary," contrary to an image of sweet and devoted Japanese mothers in earlier research reports, and that they were treated more harshly than siblings because of being the eldest daughter in the family. Holloway and Behrens speculate that this contrast between the images from prior research and the disclosures of their own interviewees may also be due to differences in social class and region of Japan between their own study and previous ones. Here again are echoes of previous ethnographic descriptions. Caudill (1963), in his study of all patients diagnosed as psychotic who were admitted to four Tokyo mental hospitals in 1958, found a statistically significant overrepresentation of eldest sons and youngest unmarried daughters, in both cases only from families that owned small businesses. In attempting to explain the findings, Caudill argued concerning a youngest daughter who was unmarried that since she had probably been pampered as a child and had reached marriageable age or beyond without meeting the challenge of separation from her family, she was likely to show the personality traits of childishness (*amaekko*) and self-indulgence (*wagamama*):

> The single youngest daughter in the family dependent on family resources [with a family business at home] is . . . likely to have an intense attachment to her father since her mother has frequently turned over to her the task of serving her father since she was a young girl—bringing him his food and *sake,* talking with him, and being a companion. Thus the *combination* of being the youngest daughter, from a family dependent on family resources, and single, would seem to be conducive for the flourishing of psychological problems. [1963, p. 38]

Caudill sets this in the context of Tokyo in the 1950s, when family-run firms were being put out of business by the growth of large corporations.

He saw mental disorder as a result of the impossible competitive pressures that small-business families faced. His account shares with that of Holloway and Behrens the assumption that the younger child will be pampered in her early years, that daughters as they grow up are assigned to take care of others in the family, and that the results can range from suppressed rage to serious mental disorder. It is not clear that there is any real contradiction between the findings of the study by Holloway and Behrens and the previous observational studies they allude to; it may be that descriptions of indulgence refer primarily to infancy and early childhood (perhaps the first three years) and the memories of strictness and responsibility to the rest of the girl's childhood. It is clear that questions of this kind concerning the emotional experience that might be hidden from standard psychological assessments require a search for deeper meanings though open-ended interviews of individuals and ethnographic observations of their early relationships.

In Chapter Three, Jin Li provides important glimpses of what the cultural meanings of learning might be that affect the experience and performance of individuals. Her exploration of the lexicons of learning in Chinese and English shows that the question of what counts about school learning is determined in part by the conceptual models of learning of a given culture that are embodied in its language. These are the resources available to parents, teachers, and pupils in a particular cultural context in terms of which they organize their own activities and communicate about educational performance. In this and the other work she cites, Li goes beyond an ethnosemantic description of the conceptual categories to elicit terms and phrases from large samples of Chinese and English individuals, indicating how qualitative and quantitative methods can work together in the explication of meanings.

While Li's approach is focused on the conceptual resources for educational participation, the analysis of Hufton, Elliott, and Illushin in Chapter Four begins with the ways in which the schools as functioning institutions generate shared assumptions and expectancies about what educational participation means. The paradoxes they identify concerning the correlates of self-perceived performance within and between student populations in England, the United States, and Russia and concerning how attributions of effort and ability are related to performance in those populations lead them to question evidence based on questionnaires alone, collect open-ended interview data, and challenge Anglo-American motivation theory. Their description of the synergy between the school environment and student motivation in Russia and the contrast they draw with the English-speaking countries raise fundamental questions of how to investigate school effectiveness. Their analysis points to the background assumptions that investigators may unwittingly share with their subjects when they fail to take a comparative perspective. Finally, the authors propose a research agenda for the future, focusing on motivationally relevant terms from the folk psychology of local populations as the cultural factors influencing the management of motivation in schools. What they call for would include the kind of ethnosemantic description that Li illustrated in Chapter Three, as well as an institutional description of the school and how it operates.

Finally, the study of Mexican American students by Quihuis, Bempechat, Jimenez, and Boulay in Chapter Five shows that the distinction between entity and incremental theorists in students' implicit theories of intelligence can dissolve with extended open-ended interviewing. With more data elicited from each student, the classification of the student becomes less clear. The authors suggest that the fuller account derived from a qualitative approach would improve the utility of the investigation for educational purposes.

Taken as a whole, the chapters in this volume illustrate the outline of a new methodology of achievement motivation: an approach that seeks to identify the cultural and personal meanings of educational performance through methods that clarify its multiple contexts. These methods include open-ended interviewing, ethnosemantics, folk psychology, and institutional description. Combined with quantitative surveys, the findings from such qualitative inquiries can be used to reanalyze generalizations based on conventional questionnaire methods and build a more valid and useful motivational psychology for education.

References

Caudill, W. "Sibling Rank and Style of Life Among Japanese Psychiatric Patients." Paper presented at the joint meeting of the Japanese Society of Psychiatry and Neurology and the American Psychiatric Association, Tokyo, May 1963.

DeVos, G. A. *Socialization for Achievement.* Berkeley: University of California Press, 1972.

Jessor, R., Colby, A., and Shweder, R. *Ethnography and Human Development: Context and Meaning in Social Inquiry.* Chicago: University of Chicago Press, 1996.

Lebra, T. S. *Japanese Patterns of Behavior.* Honolulu: University of Hawaii Press, 1976.

Stigler, J. W., and Hiebert, J. *The Teaching Gap.* New York: Free Press, 1999.

ROBERT A. LEVINE *is Roy Edward Larsen Professor of Education and Human Development, emeritus, and professor of anthropology, emeritus, Harvard University.*

Name Index

SUBJECT INDEX

Back Issue/Subscription Order Form

Copy or detach and send to:

Jossey-Bass, A Wiley Company, 989 Market Street, San Francisco CA 94103-1741

Call or fax toll-free: Phone 888-378-2537 6:30AM – 3PM PST; Fax 888-481-2665

Back Issues: Please send me the following issues at $28 each
(Important: please include series initials and issue number, such as CD90)

1.   CD_____

_____

_____

$ _____   Total for single issues

$ _____   SHIPPING CHARGES: SURFACE   Domestic Canadian
                                   First Item $5.00 $6.00
                                   Each Add'l Item $3.00 $1.50
                 For next-day and second-day delivery rates, call the number listed above.

Subscriptions   Please ❏ start ❏ renew my subscription to *New Directions for Child and Adolescent Development* for the year 2_____at the following rate:

   U.S.   ❏ Individual $75   ❏ Institutional $144
   Canada   ❏ Individual $75   ❏ Institutional $165
   All Others   ❏ Individual $99   ❏ Institutional $199

$ _____   Total single issues and subscriptions (Add appropriate sales tax for your state for single issue orders. No sales tax for U.S. subscriptions. Canadian residents, add GST for subscriptions and single issues.)

❏Payment enclosed (U.S. check or money order only)
❏VISA ❏ MC ❏ AmEx ❏ Discover Card #_____ Exp. Date _____

Signature _____ Day Phone _____
❏ Bill Me (U.S. institutional orders only. Purchase order required.)

Purchase order # _____
                 Federal Tax ID13559302   GST 89102 8052

Name _____

Address _____

_____

Phone _____ E-mail _____

For more information about Jossey-Bass, visit our Web site at www.josseybass.com

PROMOTION CODE ND3